Neon Hysteric

By Andrea Lambert

Previously Published Excerpts:

"The Warhooker Manifesto," Warhookers, 2004

"Cab Driver," Warhookers, 2004

"My Own Private 1982," "Prologue to *Neon Hysteric*," SPRAWL, 2006

"RevitaLift Night Cream," Artizen, 2007

"RevitaLift Night Cream," "Monster dot com," "Remember This," *G(u)ilt*, Lost Angelene, 2011

"Not All Naked Girls Read Kristeva," Medium, 2019

Chapter 1 — MONSTERS

This sensationalized, pornographic content is meant to be entertaining. This is fiction. None of this is true.

Hair: white, blue and silver. Crow skull at the wrist.

Let us always remember the fallen.

San Francisco: 2004.

After hours at The Rosetta Bar. A South of Market dive with no sign.

Last call rang out. The bar closed. Big Al shut the doors.

The remaining few gathered around the bar for one a last drink. I remained. The stalagmites on the ceiling shone blue like an Ice cave. Stabbing down. I sat on a leather sofa. Sipped my gin.

A blonde head rose by the right armrest. Talked. Fast.

"Hey, do you have a skate key?"

"A what?"

"I brought these roller skates and I'm about to lose a wheel. Hey, what's your name? I'm Mira." She was short. Bleached-blonde. Sharply threaded eyebrows. Expensive cosmetics on her round face.

"I'm Lena," I said,

"Cool." Shoulder-length blonde hair flipped. Her lips lacquered on. A smooth, peach tint. Lipgloss cracked. She wore no jewelry. Pink-wheeled roller skates. She was short. No drink. Electrified. Some powder or another. A black beaded evening bag. Incongruous to her casual dress. Hung from her left wrist. She switched it from left to right. Nervous.

In was dark in the bar. A neon cobra hung over the bottles. The only light. I took a drink. Considered what to say.

"Do you want to come to the bathroom with me." It was worth a try.

She smiled. Followed. Gripping my shoulder. Cautiously, so not to fall on the skates. I wondered how she made it around the club all night. Bodies packed tight together was it enough?

In the bathroom, I pulled out a small plastic bag. Dipped in a key. Offered it to her. She tilted her head. Her nostrils flared and sucked up the cocaine. Her eyes snapped open.

"Oh, but do you know what's even better? Do you know what's even better than this?"

"Shit, what?" I said. Took my bump.

"Speed! Go-fast. Have you ever done it?"

"Maybe once in a while." I would inhale pretty much anything put in front of me, at that point. It felt like adulthood.

"This stuff's a little different. Here, I've got a little bit, I'll share."

"Cool! Yeah, I'm up for it, sure." The dirty mirrors sparkled a little brighter. The red chandelier hung half-kilter above the sink. A lot of people had peed in that sink. I had peed in that sink.

My new friend laid down two tiny lines on the vanity counter. They looked like salt. A crystalline substance.

"Here. Here. Do you have a card?"

I passed her my credit card. She took it. Laid it against the crystals. Ground them in a circular motion until they were fine powder. She lined them up again. Using the flat of the plastic. There was suddenly a lot more than before. She rolled up a dollar from that small purse. Passed it to me. I snorted one line. Clutched at my face. The pain slammed claw-like through my nose.

"What the shit, Mira?"

"It's okay. It's supposed to do that. It'll go away. Here." She took the dollar from me and bent to take her line. The powder vanished with a deep influx of breath.

Her eyes snapped open. "You're going to like this, I think."

I did like speed. I liked it a lot.

The next morning at ten am, Mira called.

She said, "When I meet someone cool. "I just have to call. I hate that three day thing."

I realized that she still had my credit card.

I was still awake. Rearranging my room. Painting and making outlines for projects. Typing gargantuan plans and sparkling ideas into my old PC. I was so glad to hear that Mira had my card. I had completely forgotten about it and her.

We made plans to meet for lunch.

We met at Cafe Encore, on Post Street. Between Union Square and the Tenderloin. That space that landlords on craigslist called "Lower Nob Hill." I called it "TL, bitches."

I stood before the chalkboards. Trying to figure out what kind of panini to get. My stomach ran circles around me. I settled on a chocolate croissant.

I didn't have very much money.

"Ooh! An elegant croissant!"

"Yep. What are you getting?"

"Oh, just a macaroon. That's the specialty here. They're delicious. And coffee. Of course."

"Yes! Oh, could I have a coffee, too. Iced. Large. Thanks." I smiled at the guy behind the counter. He had plugs in his ears and a dour expression. He put a lid on my coffee. Passed me a straw.

There were three tables inside. It was morning. Two of the tables were open. We sat.

"So, Mira. I'm going to ask that question I'm not supposed to ask. I'm dying to know. What do you do?"

She fiddled with the lid of her coffee cup. Hot.

"Oh, God," Mira said. "That's hard. Like, I guess you could say I'm a housewife? A muse? My boyfriend has a job. He works at Goodwill now. Oh my god, there's so much I have to tell you. My boyfriend, my love, he was caught with other people's mail in his backpack. Like on his bike. Got in trouble. Then we got evicted when he went in jail. I've been staying in weeklies and on people's couches. My friend has been really cool about letting me stay for a few months, but yeah…"

"Oh, wow. I'm sorry. I had no idea. God, I totally didn't mean to upset you."

"Yeah, it's okay. I mean, he works at Goodwill as a condition of his parole. It's cool, like he gets first pick at the best records. I don't get to see him all that much anymore. We used to have this awesome place together in the Mission. Had parties all the time. It was amazing, but the landlord hated us."

"I think I went to a party at your place once. I remember doing E with this blond guy. Taking off. Having pretty great sex I think, of what I remember."

"Oh yeah, that was Angelina's boyfriend."

"Who's Angelina?"

"She's my best friend. You'll meet her. You guys will totally get along, oh my god, pretty girls. Just don't tell her you're the girl that did E with Ivan. She wouldn't like that."

I pulled the chocolate out of my croissant. Sucked on it. This had the makings of a total shit show.

I liked Mira, though. There was something about her that I liked. Her openness. Her manic energy. The way she so readily took me into her life. People in San Francisco were so often caught. In little poses. Delicate arcs. Conversation like minuets. They rarely confessed bold details of misfortunes, unless drugged. Even then, the etiquette was to forget it all in the morning. Even the intimacy. Especially the intimacy. Here we were, in the bald light of day. She had just told me things most people would hide like bloodstains on their pillow.

A few days later, Mira called to invite me out with her and Angelina. I was excited. I was having a friend drought. I had alienated my last party pal Audrey by seeming too obviously in love with her.

"I think you want more out of this friendship than I prepared to give you," were her last words. Toss of hair that she only had blow-dried in the salon. My type of woman was very high maintenance and very unavailable. Stone high femme? Does that exist?

So I showed up at Angelina's Tenderloin apartment. Right at the border of Union square. Liminal. Like so many things. We are all just looking in. It was an elegant building with a massage parlor next door. I tried to remember her apartment number, then called Mira.

"Oh, hi! You're here, great! I'll buzz you in."

The gate squealed. I opened it and the inner door as well. The lobby was small and utilitarian. Brown molding over beige walls. A portrait of Louis XIV on the far wall. A succession of mail slots. I realized I still didn't know the apartment number. A head popped out of the first door. Apartment 1.

Angelina was beautiful. Long chestnut brown hair flowed sideways. Past a face tilted with a querulous smile.

"Are you Lena?"

"Yes, hi."

"Come in."

She led me into a studio apartment. A Murphy bed tilted at a 45-degree angle from the wall. The walk-in closet bulged with fabulous clothes. The rest of the apartment was strangely bare. There were no CDs or records. No TV. Simple furniture. An abundance of band paraphernalia on the walls. Most of it was for Ivan's band.

Angelina was wearing tight black jeans and a sequined tube top. So was I. That was my regulation going out look. We laughed.

Angelina said, "Well, I should change something about this outfit." She disappeared into the voluminous closet. Came out with a blouse and a leather jacket. Mira and I went into the kitchen while she changed. I thought about her long, pale arms. I thought about the marks on them.

We went back in. Mira said, "Does anyone want a line before we go?"

"Oh. I brought some coke, if you're interested." I said.

"You girls go ahead. I've got something to finish up in the bathroom," Angelina said. She picked up a makeup bag from a low table. Walked down the hall.

Mira said, "Speed and coke cancel each other out. You want to do one or the other and speed lasts longer. We can do your stuff at the end of the night if people come over. Social people, they don't usually like to do speed. Oh, I forgot to tell you. Don't tell people we're doing this. It's our secret. Speed is less socially acceptable than coke."

"Ok. That's cool."

Mira laid out tiny lines. We did them quickly. Waiting. Talking. We waited longer. Angelina took what felt like an hour.

"Is she okay in there? I said. "She looked great already, I don't get it."

"That's another secret," Mira said. "She's shooting up in there."

At the Cat Club, Mira swirled in and out of the dancers. Angelina and I sat clustered close. Talked. She told me about Ivan.

"We were the most beautiful couple. People would see us in restaurants. Come up to us. Ask us if we were famous. I felt famous with him. Like we were Mick Jagger and Marianne Faithful. His band was doing so well for awhile. We were going to get married. He told me he was shopping for rings. I loved him. I loved him so much. We were doing heroin every day. His parents gave him a credit card for food and band expenses. Everyday we would go to the ATM and cash advance $100 from it for heroin for the day. It was like a dream. I was high all the time. We wore beautiful clothes. Rolling Stones every day."

"Is he here tonight?"

"No. No. Let me tell you what happened. It's horrible. It all went wrong. It's sort of my fault, or his family thinks it's my fault. They found out, of course. His parents noticed the credit card was being bled dry. Called him up they were like, what the fuck? He tried not to tell them, but his brother found out from one of his bandmates. Told his parents."

"They came down and had an intervention with him. Told him he couldn't see me anymore. I died inside. I was practically living with him. His band had bought a house in the Sunset with the money from their first advance from the record company. I was over there every day. Then suddenly, no Sunset house. Back at my apartment. I noticed little things were missing. I gave Mira a key. To just look over things. You know…"

Angelina leaned closer. Whispered in my ear. Her perfume intoxicating above the sweat and beer.

"She pawned things," she said. "Things were missing. You can't trust Mira. I know you asked her what she does. I know you guys are friends now. That's great. She needs good friends. You seem like a good person. But watch out. Don't be too naive with her. She does credit card scams. She does gift card scams. I do too. I had to once I lost Ivan. I haven't worked in years. Ivan used to support me and before that my mom did. Lately I've been scraping by on pawning things. Boosting and scamming stuff. You can steal things from department stores and return them for a lot of money. It's called boosting."

"Here, have another bump."

Without getting up, I fed it to her on the edge of my key. There were so many people pressed tight around us that no one noticed. She kept talking.

"It's nice to talk to someone who isn't in the life. What do you do, like how do you make it?"

"I temp, here and there. It's alright. I don't make a lot of money, but it's okay."

"Yeah, that's good."

"Where is Ivan now?"

"Oh." Her face crumpled. "He's in rehab. Or back in the Sunset, recording. He's not allowed to contact me."

"I'm sorry. We don't have to talk about that."

"Let's not. Let's dance, Lena. Didn't we come here to dance? Of course we didn't, but let's dance anyway." She grabbed my hand. We blended into the mass of people cramming in tiny dance floor. Hands raised. Bodies writhing. Her body against mine. Pulling away and then close and then away again.

Chapter 2 — BIRTHDAY

I lived in a rented room in the Castro. White walls plastered with pulp novel covers. Flyers from clubs I'd been to or wanted to go to. Crown molding. Gold built-in fireplace. Circular, San Francisco style bay window.

I scored the former living room of the shared flat. Draped the room in dusty brocade and books. It was $650 a month. My roommates were two gay men and a lesbian. They seemed to look down on my bisexual, hedonistic lifestyle. I wasn't sure how much longer I would be living here. Been kicked out of shared living situations before.

It was my twenty seventh birthday. I was nowhere near where I hoped to be when I turned thirty.

I sat in the window of my rented room. Watched cafe customers take tables and waiters wash them down. The mural across the street exploded with dykes on bikes. Swirls of color. Like marker pen on white paper. The whitewashed brick rainbow-lined. I watched a man sleep on a mattress against the wall.

I had few friends. Spent most of my free time hanging on the edges of things at nightclubs. Mira and Angelina, I felt closer to. Party friends came and went. According to the vicissitudes of the night.

I rang Angelina. She said she'd come over later.

I made myself some ramen. Treated myself to a half-glass of Amaretto that I bought the day before. Alcohol didn't last long in my presence. The sickly sweet almond flavor was hard to choke down.

My phone rang. It was Angelina, outside. I ran down the shadowy stairs to the door. Let her in. She looked thinner than usual. Her mouth a red smear.

"Hey. Happy Birthday! Sorry I'm so late."

"Oh, it's okay," I said. I had been waiting for her for several hours. I said, "I was just being all: brooding doom and gloom."

"Oh, yeah, almost thirty. Damn. I'm twenty seven too. I'm afraid of my thirtieth birthday."

We rattled up the stairs.

In the narrow hall, I looked both ways to make sure my roommates weren't around. They were a bit stringent lately about visitors. I let her into my room. Quickly, we decided to meet up with Mira at her SRO.

Mira was staying at the Louis Arms. The blue neon marquee stood over a somber brick building. One side flat plaster with windows carved out into the night. A fish and chips place shoved into the first floor. The lobby opened from a barred glass door to the right of the words: "Fried scallops, $5.99."

We trudged up the sidewalk to the door. Mira bent to sign us in.

"Here," Mira said. "We have to sign in guests and our comings and goings. They don't want you turning tricks here."

I looked down at the book to see that we were: "Angel-face, Gracie Lou, and Betsy Claeson." A long stretch of dirty white steps drew us upwards under fluorescent light. An old man swept the hall, slowly. Dent between his shoulders sharpened by drooping shirt. Angelina watched his back as he moved away towards the communal bathrooms. The expression on her face, I could not decipher.

The first thing I saw as we entered room #34B, was the refrigerator looming in the corner. The sharp corners over path-worn carpet. Mira had tacked a picture of her boyfriend over the bed. The limp grey bedspread marked by pink carnations and cigarette burns. The gap in his teeth. Water stains crept down the side. There was nothing else on the walls, except for a list of house rules under plexiglass. Red letters shone over a hot plate never used.

We crept in. Trapped like bugs under the bright, greenish light.

"Come on in. Here. Sit down, Lena. Do you want a drink?"

"I'll have one," said Angelina.

"I need to fix the light. This is kinda – "

"It is a bit much," I said.

Mira flicked on the lamp. Her pink scarf on the lampshade sent a rosy glow across the room. There was a smell of cigarette smoke. Dust. The eerie sweet smell of meth.

"You guys, I can't wait until I have a real place to live. I'm so sick of living in weeklies."

"Oh hey, where's the bathroom?" I said.

"It's down the hall. Shared. I would say, if you have stuff, do it in here. They probably have a camera in there."

"Cameras? How weird. No, I just have to do normal bathroom things. I'll be right back." I got up. Left.

Today was my birthday. As I walked to the bathroom I thought about what I wanted to achieve when I was thirty. I wanted to be in graduate school. I wanted to be married. I wanted to have a real job. I wanted to own a house someday. I wanted, maybe to not be a drug addict hanging out with some meth heads in an SRO.

All of my goals seemed impossibly out of my reach. I didn't know anyone who did or had accomplished any of these goals. Except: my roommate was a PhD candidate at Berkeley. He was cut from a different cloth than I. In academia for years.

I graduated with a BA in English in 1998. It was 2004. In those six years, I did nothing but drugs and office jobs. I didn't paint or write anymore. I didn't see how I could, somehow, break out of the life. Somehow become a responsible person that did normal adult things.

All I did was work temp jobs. Take disco naps. Do coke in nightclubs and afterparties. I lived for the night. I had goals, but I was avoiding them to have a social life. The substance abuse side of that social life had a larger and larger effect on my life.

I opened the little door. Went into the SRO bathroom. It was small and dirty with a small opaque window. I did my business. Left.

It was 2004. All I could see ahead of me was darkness. Cycling ahead into this demimonde underworld that I was a part of. Was a part of me. I might as well embrace it. It was all I had. As a community. Identity. I wasn't sure who I was without it.

I was one of the broken people. Bipolar. Bisexual. Underemployed. A drug addict. Alcoholic. In debt. Not a lot of options to my young life. I hung out with the people who showed me favor. I needed to hold onto the glamour. What little of that there was left.

I was so young, but felt used up. Felt like this was all there would be to life.

I came back from the bathroom.

Angelina sat on the floor. She always sat on the floor. Even in her own apartment, she slept on the floor, leaving the Murphy bed at odd angles. She said the hard surface made her feel safe.

We talked for a few hours. I was beginning to get used to the heroin, but it was still a little bit of a surprise when Angelina pulled out her rig. Mira's alcohol. Sipped. Gulped. Warm in stomach.

Angelina always talked about Ivan. Again and again. The regret. The pain. He was gone. She felt lost. She had nothing left. I watched her face.

Mira flicked on a lamp. We sat in the half-light.

I told Angelina. Again and again. There was more to live for. She would meet another. Ivan was not her only hope. She was not doomed. To live in squats. Do heroin. While his star rose. She felt doomed. To a hard life.

"Besides, I can't sing like Marianne Faithful. Ivan is totally Mick, though," Angelina said. "I don't have anything to offer except my face and my body. Fucking rock stars! They use me up. Spit me out."

"You are not Marianne Faithful. The parallel is only a parallel. It's not real. You are your own person."

"I'm not so sure."

I got kicked out of that apartment in the Castro. It all started out so well. I had to move out. I shared a place with Brady. He died. Murdered. By my abusive lover. In *Jet Set Desolate*. Jesse went to jail. No more my problem.

2003:

From the edge of Alamo Square I could see past the skyscrapers to the bay. The Victorian cupolas and turrets folded away down the hill in origami precision. I leaned back against a tree. Took a sip of horchata.

It was a week after Brady's death. I spoke with his mother about the cremation. Over awkward silences. The echoing insinuation that it was all my fault.

My fault.

Yes, in a way. I was the one who brought Jesse into the house. Enraged him to such a degree. Brady died defending me. Yes, it was my fault. I drowned in it. Deep wells of sorrow overwhelmed me whenever I looked at his empty room. Felt the silence in our flat.

The lack. The absence. A wax-dust shell around what once was and now was not. Floating away with each breath of emotion. Sadness. Love. I loved Brady. He was gone.

I gripped the paper cup. Took a milk-cinnamon sip. There was nothing that could be done. Hibiscus bloomed around me. Thrust impudent petals against my sadness. I sat up for a moment. Watched an airplane roar across the sky. Ripping through the atmosphere with rage and sparks. I was undone.

I set down the cup. Stood up to walk.

I walked. Strode through the avenues. They no longer seemed so treacherous, nor did they seem unkind. The grizzled man at the bodega sold plantains and Tampico to a young woman who held a baby close beside her. Three crackheads laughed deliriously on a blackened stoop as they passed a bottle of Wild Irish Rose. I caught a whiff of the ethanol perfume as one of them held it out to me. I smiled. Dropped down a dollar. Walked away.

I moved to the Castro right after that.

My roommates in the Castro and I were friends in the beginning. I bonded with them in the gay bars. But I liked to party just a little too much. The had school. Jobs. Lives. My roommates were uncomfortable waking up to nameless strangers doing lines in my room at dawn.

Mira called. Homeless for the last few months. She came by periodically. I let her stay in my bed. We never did anything sexual. Just speed. Talked all night. Sometimes she would pluck my eyebrows, as I was so inept at doing it myself. She put makeup on me. Took photographs that we would put on MySpace. We never got physical.

I was queer in a straight corner of San Francisco. The hipster girls around me with their asymmetrical haircuts and elegant small breasts had me in a state of constant sexual frustration.

I took care of it by sleeping around relentlessly. Unsatisfying as the men were. Young men with their polka-dotted ties and silk scarves. Not boyfriend material.

Promiscuity was more socially acceptable than making a move on one of my straight female friends. Actually taking the steps to go down to The Lexington Club to meet real dykes. Lesbians didn't much like glam bisexuals. My red crocodile clutch on the bar. Next to butches in baggy sweatshirts.

For all that I lived in a gay mecca, my rock 'n' roll cocaine scene was straight. Occasionally bi-curious if some chick was looking for attention. Wanted to make out with me only in front of people. That was all the hot girl-on-girl action I got. I was too young and short-sighted to see that satisfaction lay elsewhere.

But: Mira. She called me as my apartment share fell apart. Saved my life. As friends do.

"Hey!" Mira said, "Hey, remember how I told you I was interviewing for rooms? There's this guy, Dave, that I met on craigslist. Really stable. Nice. Responsible-type. He's renting two rooms in the Haight for $500 each. Do you want the other one?"

"Oh my God. Do you know? Do you even know? Of course I fucking do. When can I meet him? Will he care that I temp? That I don't have a real job?"

"Let's go down there," she said. "Tonight. I said I'd be there at five. I'll call him back. Say I'm bringing you. He said that if I had any friends for the other room to let him know."

"Oh my god. Thanks! Does he need a credit report? My credit is shit. Student loans and credit cards."

"Don't ask. Don't tell."

I liked Dave immediately.

"Oh, so you're a writer?" he said to me. Rumble of beats on the stereo.

"I used to think I was. I haven't written anything in a long time. I'm a very unmotivated person who wants to be a writer. Do you write?"

"Yeah. I'm trying to get into MFA Programs right now."

"What's an MFA?"

"Masters of Fine Arts, it's graduate school for writers."

"Oh, they have that? Awesome! See, this is how out of the loop I am. I graduated six years ago. I've totally lost touch with academia."

"I make puppets!" said Mira. Bounced on one foot.

"Oh, cool." His attention switched. A lock of black hair fell over one eye. "What kind of puppets?"

"Characters. Like Elvis! Sometimes I make up the characters."

"Wow, that's cool. So, do you guys want to see the rooms?"

"Yeah!"

Opening one door, he showed us a small bright room with bamboo-shuttered windows on every available wall. There was an unfortunate mural with the words, "Wall of Fame."

"The bonus to this one, although it's small," he swept a door open. "It has it's own bathroom."

"I want this one," I said.

"But wait," he said. "Until you see the other one." We crossed the hall. He opened the door. This room was huge. Mirrored closet lit by one high, small window that opened onto an airshaft.

"What do you guys think?"

We moved in the next week.

At first Mira and I shared the little room. Until another roommate cleared out of the big one. Then she moved in there. It was tight. All of our stuff piled on top of each other in that small room. We did speed on the floor. Argued in a desultory patter. Glad to have a home again. Needing space.

Another room opened up. My friend Limone moved in. On my recommendation.

Limone had long dark hair. A round face. She talked generously about ordering magazines for the house. Cheerfully suggested *Rolling Stone*. She was sweet. Open. Friendly. I was delighted to hang out with someone chill. Someone who wasn't a criminal.

Limone worked in tech now. Knew the demimonde I lived in. Still. She was there too, once. Left that life.

She and I loved red wine and cocaine. Dave bought crates of Trader Joe's two buck chuck. Regularly. Piled in his closet. We bought them off him Two dollars at a time. In quarters. Drank. In my room. Over lines. Talked endlessly.

Limone was more responsible than the rest of us. Had a job. A car. Drove to CostCo. Picked up big pallets of toilet paper. For the flat. Shared her mixed greens. Chicken patties. I leaned on her. More then I should.

I went with Limone, Mira and Angelina to The Rosetta Bar. Bordello. Amnesia. My 2004 nightclub agenda.

We piled into a cab. Headed to see Billy Vegas's band at Amnesia. Mira took the front seat. Pushed a tape into the cabdriver's stereo.

Warm yellow light from the crepe place reflected on the street. Waiters took out the trash. Wiped tables. Wire tracings of chair-backs.

I leaned back in the seat next to Limone.

"I hope this cab ride is cheap. I'm really broke tonight," I whispered to her.

"Don't worry," she said. "Watch Mira."

"Where are you from? What country?" Mira said to the cab driver. His unlined brown face like my own. Underneath all that heavy MAC foundation,

"Istanbul," he said.

"Oh cool! I've always wanted to go there."

It was a recognizable routine I had seen her take with cab drivers. Mira could charm anything out of anyone. Especially someone that didn't know her. She was a con artist extraordinaire. Mira took a few bills from the envelope in the middle seat, prattling all the time. It began to dawn on me that we would not have to pay for this ride.

Angelina wasn't taking my calls. But she wasn't taking Mira's either. Two weeks passed. We sat in our shared room with all of our combined stuff nervously piled around us. Played cards.

Mira was supposed to move out. Into the big dark room. Across the hall. Tomorrow.

It grew tense in such tight quarters. We fought. I set a stack of records on top of her video camera. I didn't know what the camera was in it's leather case.

Mira yelled at me. Stalked off into the night.

"I hope you're glad I found you a place to live," were her parting words. "I'm out. Enjoy it."

She returned half an hour later. Had nowhere to go. We were roommates again in that tiny red-curtained room off of Haight Street.

"Ivan could have called her," Mira said about Angelina. "They could be having some huge reunion special."

"But wouldn't she have said something? Called? Even just to gloat?"

"I don't know. Do you know her other friends?"

"Does she even have any other friends?" I said. "I don't know. I don't know!"

"I can't deal with not knowing. "Mira was adamant. "We should go over there. Like, even if she's not there. Or doesn't want to see us. At least we'll know something."

"Isn't that pushy?" I said.

"I don't give a shit about being pushy. She's my best friend. I'm really worried about her."

Ten minutes later, we got on the 49 bus. Transferred to a second bus. Walked past the massage parlor. Walgreens. To Angelina's place. I skip-hopped up the stairs to the gate. Punched in pound and her apartment number. We waited, tensely. Listened to the electronic echo. Cabs and cars skidded by on the street. I could feel my stomach growl.

Suddenly, the buzz came. A warm flush of joy came over me. I pushed open the door. Mira ran up to Angelina's interior door. Knocked and knocked.

"Wa-it," came her voice. Weak.

I was happy to hear she was alive. Worried instantly at the tremor.

Angelina opened the door. A skeleton. Emaciated. She let us in to cluck nervously and wrap around her.

"Honey, are you okay? We've been worried," Mira said.

"I'm going to rehab. I just can't anymore. Things have been crazy. I'm behind on my rent. I've just been putting my bills in drawers. My dealer has been giving me fronts for a while, but I'm running out of shit to pawn to pay him back. I don't have the energy to boost anymore. I just want to do H. Let everything be all warm and okay. I don't want to be here anymore. I called up my old boyfriend in Arizona last night. He was like, 'I'm going to rescue you. You can move down here. Live with me. Go to rehab. I'll take care of you until you can get better.'"

"Oh my god." I said.

"Yeah. So, like, he's coming tomorrow. He's going to help me go through my stuff. We're going to load it all in his car and I'm out. I'm done with San Francisco. I just don't have the strength."

"Is there anything we can do?" I said

"I don't know. I won't be in contact for a while. In rehab you can't talk to drug people. It might be a long time, if ever. I don't know what's going to happen. You guys. I'm so scared." She began to cry, softly, "I was so happy here. And then, I wasn't."

I already felt the same way.

Chapter 3 — MANNEQUINS

I tagged along down Haight Street with Mira. Her friend was liquidating stock. Closing up his shop. We stood outside in the blustery wind. Waited for him to unlock the storefront doors. It was around four. The ornate red and blue sign creaked a little bit in the grey breeze. "Audiophoria," it read. Black duct tape outlined the windows.

A man came to the door with curly brown hair in a pouf. He smiled. Opened the door with long arms. This had to be Ben. Mira vibrated with excitement.

"I wanted to ask you? I wanted to ask you?"

"What is it?"

"The mannequins? The two mannequins? Do you need them anymore?"

"I was just going to put them in storage."

"Can I borrow them? I work in a shop now. I think they'd really love it if I brought some mannequins in."

"Well, sure, okay."

Mira could get anything out of anyone.

Mira wheeled around the streetlight. Both hands clasped to the metal. Her knuckles strained white. Her arms were in leather. Black jeans betrayed too many Coronas. A melancholy smile lunged forwards to grasp, to devour the delicacies of the street around her. Union Square.

An ATM with yellow letters on a green awning lurked. Behind a golden line chalked on the sidewalk. Separating Mira's lamp post from the kiosk hawking cable car chocolate molds and chinoiserie by a coin-flattening machine generating an image of the Golden Gate Bridge.

Behind her, a woman with powder blue shorts shuffled forwards in powder blue Keds. Snoopy tote bag on her shoulder. Streetlights struck down.

Mira walked out of the snapshot and two doors up to the Chanel boutique. Inside, walls of ochre and black satin enfolded her in fragrance.

When she left, two ebony kohl pencils fell in the lining of her purse.

I was in the back of the car. Mira was in the front with Jeff. His arms whirled as he swerved down McAllister to Fillmore. Painted ladies with boarded up fronts. Bean Bag Crêperie. A Popeye's. A rock venue: The Independent, with its low red bulk shimmering below an iron cut-out marquee. The sun was bright.

"Thanks for the ride," said Mira. Tossed her hair. "You're a sweetie."

"Gotta help my best customer." Jeff was Mira's speed dealer.

I giggled. "Yeah, last night was awesome."

"And take good care of my Lena, right. She just needs to get home."

"Of course. I know Lena from way back. I've got a little business I need to take care of first, but I'll take her home. Don't you worry. Jeff-style."

Business. Business as usual. Mira's Business was the Haight boutique Quadra, where a mid-century white vinyl pedicure chair sat in state with a $3,000 price tag. Young couples gawked in the window, fantasizing about their lofts. Mira's business was smiling. Nodding. Cleaning the black and white checked floor. Peeling off the Twiggy magnets. Replacing them with sugar skulls. She wore clothes carefully chosen for their hipster credibility. Treading the line between "Fendi scarf as tube top, are you joking?" and "Well, if she's wearing it, it must be the nouveau vague. I guess. Where's the Whole Foods in this stinking town?"

The Stinking Rose sits in state on Columbus, North Beach, with its stained glass windows and burgundy curtains, pesto primavera and Gorgonzola gnocchi. Cannelloni. Fraying basketry around empty bottles of Chianti. They made garlic ice cream.

But I was not a waitress, as I crossed my ankles in the back of Jeff's car. After we dropped Mira at Quadra, we begin to wend our way down Laguna. Up and through the hills. My business was words, lately.

I had to get to Bernal Heights and Dustin that night. Work through the new article I was writing for Warhookers. The porn site I wrote for. I'd been twisting my lip and mauling my zits over this piece. Bent over the keyboard. Dare I?

This is the piece of erotica I was so worried about:

I climbed Mount Tam in a filmy disco dress. Stumbled heels in the underbrush. I heard rustling behind me. By the third hour I was numbed just to climbing. Not listening. Not wanting. Not knowing exactly when it would fall. Silence of this twilight. Soft leaf cover showing purple sky. I grabbed a branch to pull myself forwards. Lurched into a pine.

There was a thunder of footsteps. He jerked my neck back. Spasmodic. I felt the chill edge of a knife against my nape. The terror hit me even though I knew this could still be another crazy. He growled: "Yell and I'll cut you."

I tried to check. He gouged nails into my shoulder. Whispered tight into my ear, "Fucking bitch." He was warm and utterly alien, I couldn't know, I fell limp with fear. He dragged me, arms held, to toss against the dried leaves. The knife traced ravenously along my collarbone to slash at the dress. Steel through chiffon. Pale scraps wrecked against spider-webs. A hot spine of fear slapped through me as I saw the ski mask. Brown with red circles around the eyes.

I was naked. I writhed as he reached for my thong. Cut it off. He slapped my shoulders back down. Ran rough hands over my breasts. I curved inward to hide but was throw open as he slapped me. Fumbled with his fly.

I tried not to look at his dick as he fell on top of me, faltering. I could feel it jabbing down between my pussy lips. Thrusting inside. I gasped. He pulled back. I was dry. It hurt like a motherfucker as he hammered away in the woods, under the pine, I ground my eyes to a sparrow hopping tenuous through the needles. Tears cut down my cheeks and then it was over.

My boyfriend fell limp on top of me. The knife thrown reckless to the side. An arm wrapped lovingly around my shoulders. He rolled to the side and held me as we cried. The fury and the outrage falling cathartic as he took off the ski mask and I could see that it was him. He curled inward around my nude body. Held me as if I was the most delicate violet in a cake of candied velveteen.

That night in 2004 Dustin jogged his pen back and forth between two fingers. He took the mirror I handed him. Sniffed the cocaine. With his head tilted back, said, "I think this will work. Some women have rape fantasies. This has a boyfriend actualizing the fantasy. This was what I wanted you to write."

"It doesn't work for me and I wrote it." I said.

"You're one of those born of Mother Jones, aren't you. Steinem in the womb."

"Well, of course." I sniffed. "Why do you think I took this gig?"

"Because you were sick of fish sticks and vodka." Dustin did pay me well. Porn writing paid better then office temp work. I would take whatever work I could get at this point, sex work or no.

I said, "No, I thought you had a mission." Warhookers was described to me as a feminist site. I was a sex-positive Xennial feminist. I had thought I could get behind the Warhookers mission.

The curtains part in a small café: Paris, 1812.

I wrote the Warhooker Manifesto. I goes a little something like this:

Run with substantial female control, this site strives to depict women who are saucy and strong. Vicious and vampy. The hot ladies depicted are prime vixens. Chicks that would love to slap you around a little bit then go work on their performance art.

Our purposes are thus:

To provide a saucy yet aesthetically charged forum for women to explore and experiment with their sexuality.

To tease, tantalize, and run rampant over the nerve endings of either sex.

Through written text, to raise questions of gender, arousal, appropriateness and perversity.

To be prurient without degrading. Flagrant without withholding. Edgy without gratuitous garnishment.

To make you so utterly, deliciously, wildly hot that you come all over your keyboard.

To this we invite the viewer to transgress through the tulips and sample. It's the mating of G.I. Joe and Barbie. The union of aggression and luster. A henhouse of hedonism that invokes great shy glances and much secret running off to canoodle.

So take a look. Come on in. We welcome you.

"So, yeah Dustin, when I wrote that, and you edited the fuck out of it, I told you we were playing up the stripper goes to grad school cliché way too much. Not all naked girls read Kristeva."

"That wasn't what I said."

"Anyway. But, yeah, I thought you had this big cause, this mission. Now you want me to encourage lil' Jeffrey Dahmer's?" The night outside his attic window was streaked with streetlights. A low hum of laughter from the taqueria downstairs could be heard along with the wail of a car alarm.

"Calm the fuck down. Finish your drink."

"Do you have any ice?"

"No. I don't believe in refilling ice cube trays. It's bourgeois."

Mira stood like a paper doll against the Quadra display window. Her hands were wide on either side of her. Her co-worker draped polka-dotted scarves from her wrists and blown glass Christmas ornaments from her hands.

"Here, crook that finger up a little bit…Wait… Oh yeah! This is going to be awesome." The girl's narrow body folded to impossible postures as she climbed around Mira. Pinned things to her Pucci scarf as butterfly top.

Really, darling, safety pins only go so far.

Mira's face was slack. Her mouth half-open. Eyes blank. Her heels sunk into her Irregular Choice flats. Sinking into the floor. Anchored there.

Business. Jeff had his own business with small plastic bags. Cash only.

Last night there was only the shimmer of white hands upwards on the dance floor. Dust on the mirror of a Studio Fix as I leaned against the red streaked walls of the bathroom.

"Yeah," I told Jeff. "I'd love to see your etchings."

Last night I leaned back on a white couch at Jeff's house. My eyes were closed under sharply plucked brows. A smudge of purple shadow on the crease of one lid. My hair lay loose around my face. My lips were open in a delirious smile. Yellow teeth. Lipstick.

There were two lines on the table.

Jeff, next to me, had a handlebar mustache. Shoulder-length black hair. His leather jacket rubbed my bare shoulders. My yellow silk top draped black lace into cleavage. Or, not to say, cleavage: that blank space that exists between palm-sized breasts. Like the space between two words that strives to express.

Is it Mira, or is it me that speaks? Or are all the nights the same? It was all about that moment.

I believe in words not bodies. Not words not bodies. Not anything at all to give.

"So what do you do?" said Jeff. The car sped down a street that wasn't mine. Down through the lower Haight. Up Van Ness with the boarded up Walgreen's. Scaffolding over a pockmarked corner with homeless women huddled by the tatters of trash bags and shopping carts. Screaming up the street past the gleaming dome of City Hall, reputed to be real gold leafing the cerulean blue. I had often chewed on my straw and joked about scaling the ornate columns to the cupola and chipping it off rosette by flake.

"I'm, um, a waitress," I said

"Where?" His big hands wrapped the steering wheel with assurance. Twirling a CD on one finger, he slid it in. "Cars that Go Boom" flooded from the speakers.

"The Rose Pistola. It's in North Beach."

"Oh, you wanna go up there, get some food? You wanna get us some lunch?"

"No, I think they're closed. They're closed Thursdays. That's when they overhaul the menu and reassign the sections, I think."

I hunched over in my seat.

"No, no. That's okay."

Jeff disappeared into the ochre glow of the lobby. Spindly columns hit the pavement on either side. A smashed bottle of Smirnoff Ice festooned a condom wrapper.

Jeff revved the engine. I looked up. His lips curled in a smile. Q-ball eyes. I shivered.

"Okay I have one more place to stop at, and then lunch, and then I'll drop you home."

"I have a lot of stuff I need to go home and do."

"Well, this is what I need to get done today. This is how I make it all go. Do you want to do a bump? Perk you up a little bit?"

"Okay..." I nodded. My hands hovered above my knees. The car moved through the dense streets of the Tenderloin. Past the cracked-out maws of residence hotels. The hopeful curtains at the windows torn of sheets and dishrags.

I remembered it had been some years since I had owned at the same time paper towels, toilet paper, napkins and Kleenex to boot. Diversification of paper products was a level of adulthood that I was not up to yet.

A sodden mattress tilted against a dumpster seeping flies. A flower shop hoisted blue-dyed carnations to a cloister of men outside the M & K Market. Lucite platforms sauntered past a row of boarded up storefronts that promised, "Coming soon, Anton's tax services. A1 ASAP."

Coming soon.

Towering apartments laced with fire escapes like dead tinsel strewn reckless yet regular sped past. Each one was unique like a starfish. Jeff pulled in to an alley between Polk and Larkin. He looked around cursorily. Fumbled in his sock. Deep into the crevice between ankle and tube sock. Pulled out a bullet. Handed it to me. I wound the silver cylinder. Glanced around at the chain link. Snorted it quickly, my head tilted back. Dropping it into his palm, I shimmered. Felt momentarily, thrilled.

"So, yeah how long have you been doing this? It must be so interesting! Oh, wait, I'm not supposed to ask that. Okay, what do you want to get for lunch? I don't think I've eaten in a couple days. I keep forgetting. Things are just too exciting. Do you..."

"Yeah. Okay, kiddo. Let's go see Tonya."

I leaned against the wall in Tonya's apartment. Tonya and I were friends, neighbors and lovers in Portland in *Scaffolding*. She moved to San Francisco after me. Got really into meth. We didn't speak anymore. There was simply nothing more to talk about. Except everything, and that was too much.

The piles of disemboweled electronics in her place. Gilt-framed mirrors. My little ponies with scrawls on their faces. The remains of a pizza. Three ashtrays, one shaped like a cat. Three cats, one shaped like an ashtray. Big, fuzzy fur person. I blinked rapidly. Repressed the urge to talk.

Tonya was freaking out about something. She'd been doing meth for the last five days. Thought Jeff was trying to rip her off. He tried to convince her that a 60 was quite enough.

"No, but I'm not like other people," Tonya said.

"You're exactly like other people," Jeff said.

Tonya said, "I'm really onto something with this theory of language, I think it was the sparrows. Not speaking is the new speaking. I've got my own telepathic language that they've been telling me. I'm transcribing it. Do you want to see my notebooks? Oh wait, I've been writing in my own language. I'll read it to you."

"I think we have to go."

"Oh." Her hand twitched. She ran it through her ragged brown hair. Her white T-shirt with a sharpie-inscribed "META!" rippled above her small breasts.

"But, wait, here's another twenty if you've got some cash. Gotta help my best customer."

In front of Love 'N' Haight, Jeff whisked out the door. Yelled, "One sec!" I slouched in the grey leather seat. Picked at my cuticles. Flipped a nail along one lip gloss-smeared finger. I felt my stomach growl and flutter. The hand-lettered sign, with a giant heart hung above wide windows stuck with posters for mock duck and tempeh. Cars whizzed by around us. We were double-parked against a blue Vespa. I hoped the owner wouldn't pop out of the falafel place and key us. I lifted tense shoulders. Closed my eyes. Blinked them instantly open. Bright. Wide. It was a wonderful day.

Jeff bounded out. Handed me a warm paper bag.

"Gonna get cigarettes!" He disappeared again, this time to the liquor store on the corner. I slid a hand inside the paper bag. Pulled out two diagonally cut sandwich-halves. The wax paper revealed a moist spine of avocado, mock chicken and sprouts. I began to eat. As I ate, the jitter and the tension and the fear and the worry of the past day, the driving and the dealing and the shiver of my palms began to go. I reached into the bag. I continued to chew. Masticate. Swallow. My eyes glassily aligned with the silver Mitsubishi logo helming the glove compartment. A long glowing wail swerved from a siren around the corner. It passed.

Jeff settled both hands on the open windowsill. Said, "Okay, girl. Give me my sandwich."

I reached into the bag. Grasped at nothing. Heavens. In my fury I must have eaten both sandwiches.

How do you feel about Sun Chips?" I asked.

Chapter 4 — REVITALIFT NIGHT CREAM

Mira leaned on the edge of the Wasteland counter. Idly fooled with a rack of Chanel-C earrings. Each CC lay above a skull and crossbones. The plastic mimicked the Rosetta Bar flyers Mira and I were MySpaced that morning. In turn they resembled buttons that John handed out at Bordello two weeks ago. John's ragged blond hair around a face worn thirty-five over everyone else's twenty-two. He was culture manufacturer to a rack of overexposed ingénues. Limone and John talked close together in the club, lately.

Mira's ankles hurt. Her eyes took in the splayed silk kimonos hanging high on fifteen foot walls. Gold and crystal gowns past bound waists. Taut, seamless jeans. Below, she fingered each C and the gold chains supporting.

At the bottom of the counter a hand-lettered sign read, "No checks accepted. Credit/Debit with ID only. It's not that we don't trust you, it's that WE DON'T TRUST YO MAMA." There were red contour lines around the T's, around the M's.

Limone, Mira and I were Bordello the night before. The club was dark. A man in eyeliner shoved past my shoulder. My lips were tight.

Limone had an arm loosely around my shoulder. She wore a simple black dress and a necklace with a white guitar pick. Her long brown hair fell lush over her shoulders.

My dark hair was slicked down with pomade, around long earrings of twining gold chains. They touched the puffed shoulders of my denim blazer, above a cigarette burn. My tight gold turtleneck hugged my body, over black jeans. My hand was loose around a gin and tonic. Well gin. No ice. A neon green straw stabbed upwards against my breast.

Limone's head turned. Her lips whispered against my ear. "Hey, do you want to go to the bathroom?"

I nodded slowly. A flicker of excitement creased across my eyes. I turned to follow.

We threw all of our money and effort into nights where we strove to be brilliant and gorgeous and decadent. Then we went back to our tiny, dirty apartment. Ate bowls of cheese grits with the last of the red onion. Waited to go to sleep while the cocaine percolated through our systems. I talked. Limone talked. Mira talked. But we lost interest. Ended up lying side by side on the bed staring at the phone numbers scrawled on the wall.

In Wasteland, Mira turned to Karyn. She was ringing up a short man in a scarf.

"Hey, do you know of anything good going on this weekend?" Patter of her eyelashes against over-powdered cheeks marred by acne and the gouges of narcotic-sped nails. Blink up. She looked up.

Karyn nodded.

"Yeah," she said. "I know this girl who's doing a fashion show at the Silver Fox. We need models. Do you want to be in it? Do you know anyone?"

"Do I have to be naked?"

"No, silly. This isn't Cheetah's. Do you do scantily clad?"

"Depends on how much you pay me and if the door's left open. Drafty, no go."

"Oh, get real. No. There's no money. We will do hair and makeup. The outfits are cute. Heather Damage made them. It's her show. I think the place has a leather curtain over the door. Black. There's an awning. Come on, you know you don't have anything better to do."

"Sure, okay. Drink tickets?"

"Sure."

Fumbling through the rubble of cosmetics on the table, I plucked out the RevitaLift eye cream. Dipped a finger in the pearlescent jar. I smoothed a dollop over each eye. Glanced up. Began to pick through my hair. It hung in knives around my face. I pushed back my part. Examined my roots. Disconcerting. I was aging. There was nothing I could do. Soon, I would be thirty.

The space heater smoothed warmth on my ankles. I let the kimono fall open slightly. I pinched my arm. Pulled back a wedge of skin. A man I slept with told me he had a fetish for such things. Loose skin. Like cheesecake.

My cold sheets and take-out egg rolls were a constant. I sank down on a pillow in front of the mirror. Kneaded my hands into the red velvet.

"Do I really need it that bad?" I looked around my room to the box of condoms that had sat in the drawer for two months before opening. Now it lolled, ripped, on the bedside table.

"Hells to the yes. Apparently." I reached for the vodka tonic on the vanity table. Took a long swig.

Dustin drank a forty oz. when I got to his house. The midday sun wrecked havoc on his attic dust. He leaned back in his swivel chair. His computer was alight with a SuicideGirls screensaver.

"Lena! Wahoo, baby!" Dustin said. "What have you got for me today?"

I fell down his attic steps when I heard him. Extricated myself painfully from the steps and roller skates.

"Right. I finished the one about the Power Exchange, and the third sex tip about the etiquette of polyamory."

"Let's see it." He outstretched his hand.

"This one's called, 'How to Fuck in Small Circles and Avoid that Foul Reputation that You All Truly Deserve.' It goes a little like this."

It is right to declare yourself amoral, but don't claim polyamorous, as you open yourself to talk of earth mother malignancy. First thing to remember: You are a free frolicker. As long as you have not had "the exclusivity talk" with some smoldering amour you are free to fuck on with whoever. As long as they are not this person's best friend or housemate. Best friend's housemate, however, is fine. It's all about the degrees of separation, i.e., a direct-intense line from one of your current partners to another is bad, but a second degree is a-ok. Choice two knowing said fuck is fine. The two partaking in bathroom conferences is fine. Fingerbanging one in the other's best friend's housemate's bathroom is not. Am I making myself perfectly clear?

Perhaps I am not.

This is why it's important to keep your booty calls, comfort fucks and true yet obstinately unattainable loves separate. If you taking one home; yet see another and must grope them in the vestibule, remember that choice one will likely come up behind you and bash you in with her handbag. Well and good. Because you see, once the choice for the evening is made, it is considered bad form to reverse. Not to say it doesn't happen, but expect a little bitch-out.

Additionally, try not to talk too much smack. A bit of comparing notes is reasonable since the San Francisco sex lottery runs like a deck of cards thrown up in the air and matched. Remember that once you and your friendsters have all fucked the same ilk, the cock sizes will have been detailed and the rattiness of panties and relative palatial vs. stench of boudoir refined. After a certain point, it's all hot air for the five am coke conversation anyway, and you'll forget all the tragedies in ten years.

"Polyamory," Dustin said. "What do you know about polyamory? You haven't had a boyfriend in three years."

"Thanks for reminded me, darling. No, I specialize in the fly-by-night secret sex. They find the claw-marks later."

"Oh. I see."

I laughed. Glancing at his altar with the ritual blade and Goat of Mendes statuary. A Spanish rag doll lolled between candles.

"Oh, God. Last night he was eighteen," I said.

"Whoa! That's really wrong!"

"Like you wouldn't do it."

"I think I did a nineteen-year-old once," he said. Goat skull, toothed and sharp.

"Was it Jamie?"

"Dude, that crazy bitch came up here for a photo shoot, took all of her clothes off, and would not leave until I had sex with her. I didn't want to, I swear. She just would not stop!" Hazards of the sex industry.

"Thanks for sharing. Anyway, let's look at the material, alright?"

"This one's called, "The Cab Driver," I said. I read it to him. "Legs crossed in tart heels, tracing up to fleeting skirt. Lara rode a cab up Mission Street. It was past four am. The party sunk in absolute dreariness. She escaped without gleaning prey and was irked."

Dustin swiveled around in his chair and looked at my computer screen. Read.

The cabdriver pattered. She tuned in, "'Silent one back there? How was your party?'

"Oh, boring. Total waste of a good outfit."

"You like to party, hmmm?" She looked up from her hands. Noticed the white teeth. Benevolent voice. Accent Argentinian.

"Umm, yeah. I guess so."

"You like blow?"

She chuckled, "Sure, I like blow." This was getting good.

He pulled over. Flipped the parking brake. Moved catlike to the back seat. "Here, I'll give you a bump." He picked up a tape case. Dished out lines the size of cigarettes. White glow like calla lilies. He passed her the case. She swooped hers up whole. Leaned back for that cellophane thrill. She shivered. Watched him take two delicate sniffs.

He looked like an old friend of hers, she decided. One long gone. So not to worry when the flare exploded through her legs. He crept his hand onto her knee and further and further up while she leaned her head back in the streetlight's yellow glare. Double parked by Taqueria Cancun and rising. He flipped a hand in her panties. She sighed blissfully as he slid two fingers in. Wet.

He did look like her friend, she decided. She slid her bleached curls along his shoulder. Warm. Smelling of martinis. Her head slipped farther down to his pants, regulation brown. Shopping cart rattles down the sidewalk outside as she unzipped his fly. Slipped her hand in. Pulled his cock out. Gave it a soft, leisurely lick. He sighed. She began to suck it in earnest. Working her red lips up and down. Twirling her tongue along the purple head.

He still had a few fingers inside of her. Thrummed them on her clit. She felt the phosphorescent jangling of an orgasm hitting on. He grabbed her by the shoulder.

"I am sorry," he said. Came in a white-hot spattering down her throat.

Dustin twiddled his pen against the mouse pad. Reached for his forty. Nodded.

"These are great," he said. "We'll post 'Cab Driver' Monday with some minor edits, that we can go over now. The polyamory one? We'll wait a few weeks until your other advice piece gets more page views."

At the makeshift fashion show, the makeup artist daubed Benefit High Beam under my eyes. Smudged it across the apples of my cheeks. My deconstructed sailor suit, pared down to a halter-top and boy shorts, hastily pulled on a moment ago. I was freezing. The room, an anonymous bedroom off of Capp Street, was full of women and men in various stages of undress.

"Hey, you okay?" said some guy. Long fingers wrapped around a half-pint of Maker's Mark. He held it out to me. "Here, warm yourself up."

"Thanks. What's your name?" I said.

"I'm Travis. But wait, you're Lena, right? I think I've seen you on MySpace." He tugged at the lining escaping one sleeve, the blazer now deconstructing itself. Tan. Smooth. His cheeks were unblemished and soft. I knew instantly that I shouldn't. Not again.

The first sip of the whiskey hit me. Turned my insides all rosy.

Brush clenched, the make-up artist gripped my chin. Turned me forwards. Her lips pursed with concentration as she lined my lids with MAC turquoise.

Flat faced, I mouthed, "I go by Lena. I'm no one, really."

"Oh well then." He tucked the whiskey into a tailored pocket. The seam where the paisley ties were sewn together began to unravel. "Shit. I wonder if they can do triage."

"I think you're fucked."

"Well, you're really fucked if that starts to go."

"Oh, don't think I haven't thought of that." I pulled a silver staple-gun out of my clutch.

Motion. Light. Bodies moving around me. More whiskey. More powder. Lashes curled with a speculum. As a body, as a motion, the six women and six men moved through the procedure. Dresses. Places. Stitches. Moans. Staples. Out into the rapidly falling night.

Backstage at the Silver Fox. In a cramped utility closet. Crates of Popov and Anchor Steam. I sulked. Watched Mira flounce her golden locks at Travis.

She said, "It's all about the Blonde Brigade! Are you with me or against me?"

A woman with a botched bleach job, tendrils falling into dreadlocks and a silver clip anchoring the rest, said, "Oh yeah, baby! Oh yeah! Blonde brigade! I'm in."

"Awesome. I think if we choreograph this, it will really work."

"You have got to be kidding," I said, leaning against kegs. "This is so off-off Project Runway. I don't think we even have a runway. Come on."

"Oh, cheer up."

"No," said Travis. He peered through the indigo curtain at the smeared faces lining the bar. "We've got card tables."

"F-ab-u-lous," I said.

"Dare to dream, Lena. Come on."

"I don't know. I look weird. It's so *Querelle*."

"Well," Mira said, "I look like an Oompa Loompa."

"A leprechaun, maybe.1

"Hey!" said Mira. "No, really, green Capri pants? This jacket? Leafy? I don't care how many semesters at FIDM she has. This is so not okay."

"Look, I think we're going on. Calm down, alright. Put on a happy face," said Travis. "Do you want some whiskey?"

"You have beautiful breasts for someone of your age, Lena," said Travis, caressing one of them lightly. The blue fairy lights warred with the dawn. Outside, delivery trucks pulled up to Ti Couz.

I ran a finger across my rouged eyelid and said, "Just try to avoid that thought, shall we?"

The fog machine giveth, and the fog machine taketh away.

Chapter 5 — MY OWN PRIVATE 1982

I've written about this so many times. Written through this. Tried to metabolize.

I remember the ramen packets on the floor. In my friend Lucas' squat. The cold Chef Boyardee Ted gave me when I was hungry. The sparkly scarves. Dirty laundry. Forties of Old English. I remember the haze of cigarette smoke. The glittery collage of drag queens on the side of the kitchen counter above Lucas' bed. The floor was cement with cigarette ash. Linoleum in the kitchenette.

I remember: Reginald lay in the bedroom of the one-bedroom squat he split with Lucas. He watched me as I cut through his room to use the bathroom.

The yellowed curtains over the small open window over the sink. The cold air. The cold water. The urine stench.

I remember that the squat was in the Tenderloin. Near the ice cream parlor. Where Audrey and I had had brunch and mimosas. After the Frisco Disco formal. At The Rosetta Bar. 2003. When we were still friends. Audrey wouldn't meet my eyes anymore.

I remember: 2003. Lucas, Brady and Ted were there. I was wearing my rabbit jacket. Carrying a bottle of champagne that the liquor store guy gave me for free.

I said, "Let's drink the champagne." Ted said, "Must be nice." Economic differences ran a deep course between me and this group of friends. I came from money but had no money now. They didn't come from money and were now almost-homeless. What little I had I shared with them.

Lucas, Brady, Ted and I settled around on the low mattress. Red couch. Makeup and wine bottles everywhere. I rummaged in my clutch for the coke baggie. Laid out five lines on the coffee table. The collision was such: I always brought the drugs. I always cut the lines. I always passed around the blue half pint of Skyy, warm from a night in my purse.

By the time I left San Francisco? 2005? I spent all of my money on cocaine. Alcohol. For Angelina, Mira, Limone, Brady, Ted, Lucas, and myself. My generosity was to ruin me. But it felt so good at the time. As it always does.

By the slim light of dawn. A wallpaper collage of T-Rex and seventies pornography. Luminescent in the pale meanderings. Our collision blended to collusion. We began to spill.

Lucas spoke, "My father used to be really wealthy. He was a drug dealer in Florida. On an island in the keys. We had the biggest house in the island. With a fence and a compound around it. I had three sisters. Then he got caught. Put in jail. My mom took us to live in a trailer in Orlando."

Lucas' long eyelashes fell into eyelids smudged copper with sparkles. Long dark hair falling in his face over a torn, tight woman's shirt. He was precise in adorning the unlovely yet delectable. His long, thin body. Soft voice. Precise in unpacking the tawdry stories I had to cough up.

We all sat down at that table, did a line and coughed up a lung.

Lucas was beautiful and semi-homeless. He wouldn't go home with me alone because he didn't have hot water in his squat. He told me it was because he smelled bad. Didn't want anyone to know. He hid that with signifiers of fabulousness. Androgyny. Glamour.

Lucas and Reginald were kicked out of the squat for throwing a party. Lucas was homeless. Reginald went to New York. Became famous. Lucas called me years later when I was in grad school. Told me he was washing dishes at his sister's massage parlor.

When I think about the collision of communities, I think of both collision and collusion. When I first met Lucas and started hanging out with him, Brady and Ted, I was young thing who worked in accounting. In my late twenties, my novelty as a writer who talked about her work in clubs faded. My finances bled. I lost many jobs. Began starving.

These feral kids took me in. As the hipsters cast me out. The sharp hips and red lips closing to the squalid flats and endless nights with these street kids. They lived more vividly. Than the blank eyed nosebleed queens I used to know.

2003. A spring night in San Francisco. Past the squat's concrete slab for a yard. Pale green hallway with a flickering bulb. A man speaking in Portuguese a long way away. We would shuffle in once Lucas flopped in through the window. Unlocked #14A from the inside.

Brady was HIV+ and on SSI. Brady and Ted were lovers.

There, within the totalizing effect of the cocaine, our divisions were forgotten. We began spilling bloody stories. Some of mine were as bad as their's.

I remember running out for a Chili Relleno burrito. As morning became clear. We roused ourselves from the couch cushions and the floor. I remember coming back. Sharing it with Lucas.

I sometimes wondered if they would still hang out. If I didn't come with wine and coke. When I ran dry. Broke. Started coming with neither. They were still there for me.

It was all along the water. Except there was no water. There was only the concrete of the sidewalk with the shards of King Cobra bottles and burrito wrappers. Brady, Limone and I walked down the lower Haight towards home. The haze of mist hovering in the air rose. We halted.

I leaned on the edge of the bus shelter. Shoulders bent from too much. Too soon. Too far. Too far away from what I really wanted I traced our route on the bus map. Looked up at the hidden sun that left a dim glow over us.

I was twenty six. Young in action, but fearing the clock. The years since I left college drifted behind me. I painted idly. Temped even more carelessly. Went out with the most vigor since Waterloo.

The bus screeched to a rocky stop in front of us. Lights on. Brady entered first. He flashed his disability pass.

The bus computer intoned, "Seventy-one. Haight Noriega. Thirty-sixth avenue and Ortega."

Brady was twenty-five. Gay. A gentleman in his velvet jacket with blue roses embroidered on the lapels. He tossed his cigarette onto the sidewalk in front of Naan and Curry. Shuffled down the aisle to a seat in the back.

Limone climbed the bus stairs easily. She was robust with long chestnut hair. She leaned back to lend me a dollar for bus fare. Back then Limone lived with her socialite parents in Marin. She came into the city to see me. Enjoy the nightlife. Her website was the highest concern in her life. Mid-wifing it into being. With the same care that she gave to a dusting of rose shadow. Or a basil seedling.

In the dour evening, we rode up Haight Street. Each thought our own thoughts. Each more surely wrapped in confusion. The bus rumbled to a halt. When I set my feet on the ground by the Happy Donut, I felt it even more surely.

Whatever it may bring, let the night begin.

2004:

I wrote porn to eke out a living. Was in fashion shows. Volunteered at my friend's art gallery. It was the last time that one could live in San Francisco without a real job. I would be homeless now. Had I stayed.

I volunteered at Janey's gallery off and on. I was over there one afternoon in 2004.

"Slap self infant instance succession," droned the video diorama. An image of a pained-looking woman doing aerobics. I stared at it. Wiped the Clorox wipe across either black-dusted corner of the pedestal. From my peripheral vision, Janey flipped her car keys on their green elastic.

"Okay," Janey said. "I'm going out, I'm going to BevMo to get stuff from the opening. If anyone wants to buy anything, get their name and number and say we'll call them back."

"Have you ever sold anything?"

"No, "said Janey. That's why I have a day job,"

The gallery door slammed behind her. Light drizzle gave way to overwhelming clouds.

I hoped it would be clear tonight. Better turnout. I stared out the window at the ragged panorama of Valencia Street. Down past 16th, the Mission turned to furniture boutiques and sushi. Korean BBQ. A high prevalence of yuppies driven in from the Marina and Marin to park their SUVs on the center divider. A $50 ticket meant nothing if you had reservations at Rambla's.

On our corner of Valencia, Janey and her boyfriend rented a storefront. Crudely painted it green. Named the gallery "Swamp: a Place for Activism, Art & Ideas."

The immense, abandoned brick armory separated us from commerce into a world of bombed-out liquor stores. Kink.com made Internet bondage porn in that armory in the twenty teens.

2004. Valencia and 13th was scrawled-out shop windows. Struggling coffeeshops where homeless people spat in your quiche.

I wiped the chemical wipe across the sill of the front window. Glanced down at the weight of soot it accumulated. Glanced outside momentarily at the homeless man rearranging his mattress. Turned inside. Where the 'zine library's decade worth of queer teen angst awaited me in courier 12 pt font.

Lucas was up against an eighties movie poster at my apartment. I took the photo. His green doe-eyes rimmed in teal sparkly shadow. Pink glowing his lips. His light brown stubble extended down his neck. Up to long, greasy hair that undulated across his face. His black jean jacket bound an open-necked sparkly rag. Cut in places where tufts of hair stuck out.

He looked down. Dimpled. Looked away.

Lucas rode in Critical Mass. The communal bike ride that activists had through San Francisco. His skinny legs cycled fast through the night. He looked up to see the lights of Taqueria Cancun streak by. Thought about a burrito. Discarded the thought.

He'd have to lift one off an outside table anyway, as he had no money. It would make him lose the group.

He sped down Mission Street with the horde of cyclists. Blocked all traffic. Turned up to the 16th Street BART Station.

It was dark. The faces of the tourists, prostitutes, dealers and randoms flashed past him in phosphorescence. He drew his black sweatshirt down over his head. Looked down.

At the intersection of 14th and Valencia, outside the Swamp, I texted Lucas: "Are you coming? There's beer!" I tucked my phone back in my purse. Blended back into the opening crowd. Spilling across the sparkle pockmarked sidewalk. Dropping cigarettes and damp plastic wineglasses.

I was volunteer bartending. I had "a job to do." All of this volunteer work looked great on a resume. Social. Kept me involved culturally. Around people that were not heavy users.

I folded my way through the crowd. Gave a nod or a smile here and there. Pinched Mira on the shoulder as she stood slack-mouthed before a gigantic movement-activated insect. The art installation's lights, pulleys, gears and sound loops responded to the motions of the people in the room.

Mira said, "Oh hey, do you have any – "

"You… You… Rattle… Buzz… You." Emanated from the blazing eye.

"I gotta work." I said. "Come talk with me at the bar if you want."

"Want… Buzz… Work… Bzzzz…"

Guy Debord states in *The Society of the Spectacle* that "the spectacle is not a collection of images, but a social relation among people, mediated by images."[1] Mediation of canvases and mechanical cockroaches.

The urban location. Curtains open. The sequin tube top. The strobe. The plastic wineglass. The head turned sideways with regard. The cruel and crucial fragile empathy.

Are you really listening to me?

The night before, I stood on a ledge in the silent lilac street with the party upstream. Watched the pretty things with Limone and Lucas.

"So I was giving my friend a blowjob in his car today," said Limone.

"Driving?" Lucas asked.

"Car parked, stupid. While I was finishing, Lena called. Of course it would be Lena to call me at a time like that. Then I was getting the phone, and I had cum all over my hands. It was all sticky and nasty…"

She laughed with a flash of lipgloss.

Lucas said, "So I was walking up 19th street when this dude picked me up. He wanted me to suck his cock. I said okay. So I was doing it. The guy was slamming my head up and down. Saying, 'Yeah, you'll be one of my bitches. I'll pimp you out.'" Then I threw up all over the guy's dick and balls and -,"

"That probably really turned him on," Limone said. "All warm and wet down his butt crack." We laughed.

Scent of gardenia and twilight. A blonde from the upstairs window yelled, "I know you all want to party, but I've got a kid up here trying to sleep…" We drifted down the block. Melted into the street.

Mira and I were still at the Swamp.

Mira followed me. I traced to the back of the gallery. The dim light broken by a spotlight. Janey popped busy bottles of Sierra Nevada and Pyramid Ale. Pressed them into the hands of men and women milling around in front of the tiny white-paneled kitchenette.

"Wait a sec." She turned. Rummaged in the refrigerator two feet behind her by the blue plastic bucket of ice-bound bottles. Pulled out some teriyaki braised tofu and sesame thins.

Janey said, "I need some space. Are you ready to take over?"

"Yeah, sorry about that." I said.

Janey fell down into the handmade wood chair behind us. Began slicing her tofu. The savory brown exterior fell easily to buttery insides. She ate. Lifted and carted her snacks towards the tiny loft space above the gallery that she shared with her boyfriend. Climbed up the crude ladder. She lunged. Fell headlong into the four-foot space. The avocado ahead with knife.

---

[1] Debord, Guy, *Society of the Spectacle* (Detroit: Black & Red, 1983) 4

A cough, and the heroin balloon was in the man's hand. Slightly mucosal. He palmed it to Lucas. Lucas slipped $40 into the man's other hand.

The BART rushed under beneath them with a low, rumbling sound. Barely heard between the heaving buses and cabs with sure agendas darting between cars like jaundiced flies.

There would be bumblebees, if there were bumblebees here, but here there was only the crabgrass on the chainlink around used car lots. Silver graffiti on Spanish billboards.

Adelita's Cake Con Sabore shuttered their windows. A loose dusting of powdered sugar on the curb, where a pink box lay half-open. A few cuernitos and bits of pastel de tres leches lay there, nibbled. It's a long journey from the flour to the lip.

Lucas kicked the box. Walked his bike. The pedal scraped his leg under his purple pants. He pulled out a cream-filled empanada. Bit resolutely on one tip

There were no stars but the dual stars. The lines of the streetlights and headlights as they stretched past him. Lucas got back on his bike. Rode away.

Behind the bar, I set both legs wide apart. My boots heavy over my knees.

"Okay," I said. "Who wants one."

"Oh! Hey? I'll have the red." I looked up to see blond fuzz over a shaved head. A graceful elongated scalp. A red leather jacket that echoed Michael Jackson in such heavy irony that I took it as intentional. His wide blue eyes blinked, open.

"Hey, you're that graphic designer I met with last week, aren't you?" I said. "I recognize the head."

Mira rolled her eyes from behind the bar. She drank white wine. Nibbled on a leftover piece of tofu. Raised her eyebrows at me.

Well. I was taking care of my own needs before hers, today.

"So that was you," the bald guy said. "Yeah, what did you think of the flyers? I felt they were a little too digitally driven, I tried to make them more organic, but – "

"But it's fundamentally an electronic show. I mean, check out that one…" I gestured with his beer at the sound-loop cockroach.

"Right, right," the new man said.

Chapter 6 — MASSAGEZ MOI

Two hours later.

The long line of palms bisected Dolores Street. The burn of exhaust on my left calf. Bare. My thighs tight on Red Leather's body. My hands woven tight around his waist as we sped down Dolores on his blue Vespa. I breathed in gulps of brisk exhaust-filled air. Prayed that we wouldn't turn too fast as we wended around a corner. Dipped into the curve.

"Lean with me," he said. I laughed.

My phone beeped. Likely Lucas. It was going to have to wait. A few streets later, the iron gates and piles of plaid rags, discarded Papasan's, and stunted trees woven intricately with yarn and photographs passed by. My phone beeped again, than began to ring.

"Shit, they must want me bad." The wind took my hair from the helmet. We pulled over.

"I guess I did say, it was only going to be around the block," he said.

I pulled my white vinyl coat tighter around me. Wrapped my arms around him again. We swooped. Approaching Valencia, I saw that the street was completely blocked by Critical Mass riders. Bicycles streamed torrentially. Stopped all traffic.

The protestors chanted quick blurts of, "Bikes not Bombs!"

"Free Mumia!"

"SUVs out of Iraq!"

"Reclaim the Streets!"

I laughed. This happened every Friday. Nothing to do but wait. Watch the strain of nubile calves. Go to Zeitgeist for a beer. After the spectacle. Where the riders would be decompressing, too.

"Hey, let's double back and go up 14th," I said. "I think the bar's still open."

"No, let's ride along the sidewalk and watch. I love this shit."

"Hell, no, we won't go!" Roars and upraised fists.

"You do realize you are part of the oil-industrial complex? This sucker doesn't run on canola," I said.

"Hey," the guy said. "I shop at Rainbow Grocers... I'm vegan..."

"That's great. I wear fur but I got it at Goodwill so it's okay. Besides, I spent my last $10.00 on it. So I'm ghetto fab, okay. Don't mess with it."

"Really, it's fine Do you want a tissue?"

"Do you want to go into the alley for a sec? I've got some shit."

"Sure."

The supple leather of his jacket slithered through my fingers as I slid off the Vespa. Fumbled in red croc-skin clutch for the baggie of blow. I held the key out to my guy's nose. He inhaled sharply. Jerked his head back. The dust on my house key glowed against the darkness of the brick steps we were sitting on.

"Do you realize how bloody this shit is?" he said.

"You can stuff your hipster oil rig where you know you want it as long as you are doing my shit," I replied.

"Fine, just so you're aware."

"Do you want another?" I said. I knew how this worked.

"Um….yeah!"

"I though so."

We heard the roars and chants of the protesters to the right of us. Loud. Angular. The whirs of wheels rang sharply with our absence.

Eyes bright. A bitter drip in the back of my throat.

I said, "Do you think we should get back, it's sounding a little – "

"Clear this intersection on the double. This is precinct 4-16. I'll give you a count of 10," came the policemen's bullhorns.

"Oh, fuck!" We leapt up on the scooter. Hands gripped tighter. I leaned incoherent to his warm body against the loud, rapidly chilling night.

We squealed up Dolores. Bright mirrored murals glowed. Bay windows reflected our passage. We turned to wheel up 14th towards Swamp. I heard the whine of police sirens. The thuds of marching horses behind me.

"What?" said the guy.

"Come on!" I said. We squealed up towards the gallery. Just in time to stop where the opening spilled into complete mayhem. Activists and art people huddled inside the building. Muddy mountain bikes wedged tight in the entryway. Litter of brown bottles and cigarettes on the pavement in front. A group gathered there.

"Ain't no power like the power of the people, and the power of the people don't stop!" someone yelled.

I could see red flashes of the police cars. The sirens cascading. The many-colored faces blaring and separating in front of me.

"Look, I've got to drop you here," said Red Leather, lifting me off his scooter.

"What the fuck?"

"No, listen. My girlfriend will be really upset that I stayed out this late. I can't let her know that I was part of this...." he sniffed.

"You're just going to…?"

"You have my card, right?" he said. He sped up Valencia towards 13th and the freeway overpass. I saw the brisk aqua blur speed through and away.

"Fantastic." I turned. Scrabbled at the Swamp door. Tried to get them to let me in. Packed tight. Terrified. No one would open the gates. Locked down. I turned. Looked back to where the riot squad had turned in on all three fronts. A pile of bicycles in the middle surrounded by a circle of people.

"Shit." I turned. Began running up Valencia towards the overpass. Someone overturned an SF Weekly dispenser. Lit the newspapers on fire with a loose bic.

I pelted. Heels teetering. Nights running drunk across traffic taught me how to walk so encumbered. With the whiff of smoke, a second spray of teargas came across my back.

There was a photo of Limone and I up on The Rosetta Bar's MySpace page. Brisk behind smiles. Limone tilted a glass of white wine to her mouth. My fingers clenched around a gin and tonic. Well gin, no ice. My drink. Our nearly identical low black tops hid shimmer and came to a point. Colors laced behind us on the black wall. Our faces caught the light pale like flecks of cocaine on a CD I thought was clean. A last baking soda starlight.

"Fuck." I said. Tear gas. It had been a long time since I was in a riot. Not since the Seattle WTO riots. 1999. An terrifying experience. I hoped to never repeat it. I fell to my knees. The white vinyl jacket smeared in the mud. The middle of my black cashmere scarf fell into a puddle of rainwater at my feet. All around me, people dropped. I felt an arm on my shoulder. Wrapped the wet spot around my mouth and nose. Teargas trick from the WTO.

If you wear something with enough confidence, people will think it's high fashion. If only in a highly ironic way, further heightened by your astute cultural sensitivity. But always Thrift Town. Never Urban Outfitters. A sensitivity to the passionate rat-a-tat-tat of the blood pulse. Right? That they, of course, just don't quite get. It must be them! Their lack of a pure sense of irony to understand that scarf. Right?

At least that was what I told myself, as I plunged into Bordello. Self-conscious in gold sequin tube top. This is our own private 1982. Believe it, babies. A nineteen year old Art Institute brat in the black lace high collar blouse blinked cocaine eyes at me.

"No, dear. It's my own private 2001," she said.

It's 2004. I don't even know anymore. I'm terrified.

Is it Limone who talks, or is it me? Are all nights the same? We fucked again on speed after Bordello. We had that kind of relationship, sometimes. It became pyrotechnic; at least for a few minutes, in front of the mirror. I threw aside the blue vibrator.

"Were you faking that?" I said.

Limone curled up. Shivered still.

"What do you think?" she said. "I don't fake it. That would give you the wrong idea. Up, not down. Left, not right. Pyrotechnic."

Sparks and stars and fireworks. Sparklers in some disremembered Reno Forth of July. Held by little boys who may or may not shoot their eye out. I blinked and thought about the family I didn't call. The weddings I didn't go to. The dress with long tattoo-hiding sleeves that my family wanted me to buy. To stand in the crowd and avoid the bouquet.

Terrified as another wave of teargas hit my eyes, I saw Lucas crouched on the ground. He bunched his muddy hair across his mouth.

"Oh, hey." I said. "I think you missed the art fuck."

"Let's get the fuck out of here." Lucas said. "I think I lost my phone."

"Where's your bike?"

"Behind a dumpster of 15th."

We fumbled our way upwards. Began to run. People and bicycles came roaring around us. We reached the corner where Valencia eased into Market.

Lucas said, "Well, as the route to your house is basically en inferno, do you want to come over?"

"Yeah, that would be nice." My eyes above the black scarf. I was still breathing through it. My eyes were red and watery. I bent to cough. Gasped.

 Lucas took me by the shoulder.

"No, really," I said. "It's cool. I can walk. Really. Don't hero me."

Lucas and I were at his squat in the Tenderloin. Thumps of a DJ came down from the party above. We wiped mud and teargas off our faces. A few sofa cushions and an old mattress were tossed on the bare concrete floor. Packets of shrimp ramen and a couple forties of Olde English were scattered there. A glittery scarf laced them. One of my kohl eyes dipped as I did a line off a Mutilated Mannequins CD.

 "My sister wants me to work for her." Lucas said.

"Where?"

"Massagez Moi"

"Is that massage plus?"

He sighed. "Yeah."

"Wow. Are you gonna do it?"

"No. I mean, not unless I have to. Maybe. She said I could start by washing dishes. Being a security guard, kinda."

"You're 5'4""

"Well, I guess we'll just have to hug it out, then. Whatever they'd prefer."

I sniffed. "I'm sorry, honey. Do you want a line?"

"Actually, wait, I've got something better." Lucas rummaged in his jean pockets. Thumped the balloon onto the mirror. He glowed from the inside. Like a sprinkler on a sunny day.

"Oh, that shit. Sure. Do you have any needles?"

"Let me look. I think I do," he turned. Began sorting through the drifts and eddies of small black garments. "Shit. Wait, over here. On my vanity." He rustled through drawers. Pulled out scraps of paper with numbers written on them. The odd empty baggie slit down the side. Can after can of Chef Boyardee. Setting a tub of wet and wild Sparkle Kraze on the floor by his beer, he delved into the last drawer. Came up empty.

"We can get one on Turk and Eddy," Lucas said. "Maybe as far as Civic Center."

"Are you sure about this?" I said.

"No, really. I've done it before. Really."

"Okay. Let me take my this off." I slid my grandmother's gold watch into my purse. Tucked it into a corner by the mattress. Bare and stained.

That was the last time I ever saw that watch. I never knew if Lucas or one of his roommates stole it when I was high. I never asked.

We walked four flights downstairs.

Lucas took my arm as we slid out the gate.

I said, "You're hero-ing again."

"Sorry." He dimpled. Looked down.

"Outfits, outfits," Lucas said. Prowled the corner of Turk and Eddy with me on his arm. We walked up Turk to the Canon X parking structure. I saw what I took to be mannequins left out from some art project. Getting closer, I saw that they were transvestite prostitutes. Vinyl skirts cocked at odd angles against the chain link.

The shuddering slatted fences hung diagonal against the concrete walls. It was four in the morning. All the street angels posed. Black and white scalloped minidresses along the chain link. The chain link. One of the hookers leaned forwards. Poured forth the syringe in her hand.

"Here, baby."

Lucas's hand shot out. He took the needle in a sleek, sly motion. The street was dark. Open. Empty. Barren black rubble of the asphalt sliding over the ground. No teeth.

The needle hovered over my forearm. My pale skin behind my elbow touched with purple pinpricks and blue smudges. I wasn't much of a junkie. I didn't do this often. Heroin was never my thing. Let's just say I've tried it. The ochre light in the room hung heavy in a black lantern.

"I heard someone say the cops were tying people to the guide rails of the bus with cable ties," said Lucas.

"Can you believe everything you hear?" I said. I pressed the needle into my damp skin, without penetrating.

"He was in Earth First."

"Right. Scooter-boy was vegan."

"That's great! I'm vegan."

"That's great. I buy budget steaks with change."

"Oh my God." Lucas said.

"No, really, they're not bad. Even the worst steak crusted with pepper and two-buck-chuck is yummy." I cooked them up night after night in the apartment I shared with Mira, Dave and Limone. One wafer-thin budget steak every few days became all I ate in my welfare queen poverty.

Lucas leaned forwards over the spoon. Dissolving the tar and powder. I focused. Clenched my teeth. Slid the needle in. I missed blood. Poked around instead in the painful blank tissue. Infertile in the orange light. Lucas clicked off the lighter.

"Shit!" I exhaled between my teeth. Grit them again. I pumped my fist. Tightened the pink scarf. Stared fiercely at my arm. I wasn't very good at shooting up. Veins too small. "Okay." This time the point hit blood. I pressed the syringe slowly as the long tendril of red came up.

The warm, lush wave hit me almost immediately. I fell back on the mattress. My hands slack. Let the needle sit ensconced for a moment while the pleasure webbed through me. Lucas beside me.

Finally, I slid the syringe out. Set it limply on the coffee table next to his. His and hers like towels. Soft pink and blue fluffy towels that my mother would wrap around me fresh from a hot bath. With dahlias and magnolias falling from my hair into an expanse of rabbit fur.

I ran a hand across Lucas' soft, long hair. Smiled. In the end times.

At home, the next day, I pawed through a pile of books. My hair askew. My hands dry with cracked, dirty nails. My desk at the Haight apartment was a rickety white and gold princess desk from the seventies.

From Thrift Town. Tied it into my old Honda with twine. Black dress stark. Against a single glass of red wine. In a blue goblet. With molded grapes. The ever-present wineglass left burgundy rings. On the coffee rings. On the dust. On the croissant flakes. On the desk. On the desk were books. A Dell PC. *Powers of Horror* by Luce Iriguray.

A horrifying picture of my own loss of faith. In the words I typed. In the proper words. In the final footnote.

In the letters of my name "Lena Cosentino" that spelled in anagram "Lost lone toil in innocent neon sin. Stolen tinsel consent." I did consent, to all of this.

Chapter 7 — THE SERRANO HOTEL

From my seat at the back of the 38 Geary bus, I could see every stitch in the stripper's bra. I assumed she was a stripper, anyway. Flamboyant thighs dripping from a spandex miniskirt. Bra straps lolling from an off-the-shoulder top.

I wouldn't judge. My pink chiffon scarf wrapped silky and dubious around my hair. I was visiting my new acquaintance, Tank, in the Serrano Hotel. His voice on the phone intrigued me. Gruff. Low. Inviting me to room #1455. It was registered under the name "Joseph Ernst."

With a dull evening ahead of watching the ceiling fan shake as it spun at home, gilt curtains and mini-bars enthralled me. No matter that I had met him two days ago. After a night of E, I made out with this bald man missing a tooth. He invited me to his hotel room tonight. I decided to go.

I felt ready for anything. Up for adventure. I got one. It was to poison me clear out of town.

"Fuck," sneered the stripper on the bus. "I have to get to work on time. You're going way below the speed limit!" The driver scowled. Cars staggered through the Market Street traffic. Bleared angry honks at the bus stalling at every stop. Labored like a pregnant woman with a missing limb to crawl past Civic Center Station. Furious neon from the strip clubs screamed of delights impossible. Unreasonable. Truly concerning your immediate attention.

"I'm going as fast as is reasonable, lady. Try walking."

"No, you're lagging so bad. Let me out, here. No, let me out. I've had it with this." The woman reared on angry motorcycles boots to stomp off the 38 Geary and out into the night. It was suddenly very quiet. I drew my leather jacket closer. Two more stops.

"Union Square!" exclaimed the driver. I lurched up. Reeled. Climbed down the stairs to the street. There was a glacial sheen upon the shop windows as I trotted up Powell Street. The flower cart with the gardenias boutonnieres was shuttered and bare, Urban Outfitters let forth a dim haze of thinly veiled cliché. The cable cars were thankfully defunct. Quiet. All mine. I laid a cautious finger on the railing of the cable car roundabout. As if it would hurt to encroach. Nothing bit back. I slid my fingers around it. Ran them along its length. Watched the copper oxidize with filth.

I let my hand fall from the railing. Turned upwards to the opalescent span of the streetlight. I felt so isolated in this city. Grappling through the days. The gleaming shelves of lip gloss palates and plasticized Dior in the Sephora window just confirmed this. Looking promised so much. Left me still alone. Still outside. Still left behind. I paced up the long street to the gleaming mass of the square. Equally pristine and barren.

I pressed my lips together. Tried to shake off the feeling of unease. Moments later, I stepped up the curb and onto the sparkling concrete outside The Serrano Hotel. A doorman in a bow tie swept the door wide. I strode in. Approximated the sort of dignity I had learned gets you far on no credentials.

"I belong here. I have stayed in many places like this. I am visiting a friend. It is all perfectly legitimate. No, I am not a hooker." Just about to trade sex for drugs. As one did in clubland dating. I was game.

I used to trade sex for food. Dating is inevitably transactional. So are friendships. That's how it works. Or is that always how it has to work?

Do all relationships hinge upon mutual consumption?

Are those only the toxic ones?

Is there another way to live?

The lobby was marble and mirrored. Reflected velvet ottomans and a gargantuan fireplace. Tiny, piquant streaks of flame went darting across logs like fingernails on thighs.

It was absolutely quiet, except for a "Click. Click. Scratch." My nail-worn heels tip-tapped across the parquet. Layers of slotted, glossy wood pressed up at me.

I shot my eyes straight ahead. Past the concierge. To the red lacquer doors of the elevator. Framed in black wood. The squares above and below bisected me into concern. Confusion. Disruption. The continual dissonance of what was I doing here? Where was that room number? What exactly was my agenda with this trip, anyway? I rustled in my purse for the scrap with Tank's information. Peered anxiously over my hand.

The elevator rose. Trapped me with a low, whirring roar. With a resonant tone, the doors parted. Releasing me. Into a hall wallpapered in cream with gold-whorled lattice. I wavered. Glanced at the floral arrangement on the pillar. Turned from one door to another. Room #1455 was before me. The "Do Not Disturb" sign hung at jaunty angle.

I knocked. Lightly. Harder. The door creaked open to reveal Tank with a drink in his hand. His baldness shone with grease. His stubby hand raised in greeting. He smiled impishly. Revealed the missing tooth. In the amber light of the hotel room, the home-done tattoos seemed forgivable. I realized Tank was once quite attractive. Thirty-five years and heavy speed use had left its mark.

I was twenty-seven. In the arrogance of twenty-somethings, I assumed was superior to anyone older than I who was still living this life.

My eyes strayed over Tank's clothes, but research was unforthcoming. I knew how my roommate Mira used credit card scams to her advantage. Possession of designer clothes was often less a matter of disposable income then disposable morals.

"Hey, come in." Tank beckoned me. Backed away into the warm cream womb of the room. I slunk in. Took off my pink scarf. Set it on an end table. I looked past him to see the bed: huge. A massive cream down comforter in red and white. Gold pillows streaked with incoherent French. Tank poured me a rum and coke from the mini-bar.

Under the sweeping arch of the valence, it seems rude to ask how the room was financed. Stolen credit cards, again, most likely. I knew how Mira's people did things by now. Tank was a friend of hers.

I took the meth pipe from him hesitantly. Put it to my lips. Flicked erratically with the lighter. The blue flame licked the glossy smears of speed. I sucked cautiously. Breathed out a cloud of chemical smoke. A warm luxurious feeling fell over me. I watched the city shimmer from behind the double-paned windows. Lay back on the bed.

"I'm not going to make out with you. I hope you know that," I said.

He stiffened, his arm behind me.

"That's a little abrupt."

"Well, you know. Last time was kind of a fluke." I pressed my lips together mincingly. Shrugged.

"You're really winning points here," he sighed. "Me and my ego will just be going now, thank you very much."

"Not cute."

"Girls like you always treat me like this." He nodded bleakly.

"Girls like what? How many girls do you take to your hotel rooms on a weekly basis, anyway?"

"That's not fair. Do you want another drink?"

"Oh yes. Thanks."

He mixed it deftly and handed me the snifter. I swirled it slightly. Took a sip. Set it down. He pulled a coaster from a drawer. Lifted my glass. Settled it softly to the cork.

"There, all better now," I said.

"Well, aren't you special. Hey, listen. A friend of mine needs to come over to get some checks I'm making for him."

"Checks?"

"That's what I do. I make fake checks and fake IDs."

"Aha. How did you start out?"

"I used to be a bartender, back when I lived in Petaluma. Then I moved down here to the Tenderloin. Started bartending again. My girlfriend of five years and I, we had a daughter. I had to make more money for the kid, so I started doing this. My friend Jeff started me on it. First little stuff. Faking a postmark or a used stamp. Then harder until now I can do a California ID, no problem. Wanna see?"

"Wait, you have a kid?"

"Here, here, let me show you." He flipped open his laptop to show a screen saver montage of a child's face. Tiny. Teeth gapped. She was elfin with fine, light brown hair.

"She's what I live for. She's why I'm still in San Francisco, because my baby momma wants to live here." Tank said." When she goes, I'll go, too. But we broke up when Sunny was two. My baby momma got custody. Now I hardly ever get to see my kid." He looked up at me. Eyes welled.

I patted his shoulder. "It's okay."

"Yeah. Whatever."

There was a heavy knock. A big man swung open the door. Obese in filthy brown overalls. Beard stabbing over an open collar. He thumped down in one of the damask chairs. Rummaged in his bag for a pipe. Pulled out a meth pipe. Handed it to me with a lighter. Grunted at Tank.

I flicked the lighter. Watched the speed drip down the side of the glass globe. Inhaled.

Tank pulled a package of checks from a deep oak drawer. Handed it to the man. He took it. Put a wad of twenties in Tank's hand. Turned to go. When he was gone, Tank turned to me.

"Sorry you had to see that," he said. "But you see, I gotta do my business."

"It's okay."

"No, really." His eyes softened.

He reached out and cupped my shoulder gently. I leaned back. Closed my eyes. Gave up for a moment. The vast gilt mirror reflected my eyes, closing, as Tank moved in.

Back home. The next morning. I threw my purse down on the kitchen floor. Dodged over to Mira's room. Our dirty five bedroom flat. In the Haight District of San Francisco. Was full of co-existing drug addicts. Everyone did something. As we all did different things? It worked out. It was one of the last times in the twenty-first century when people could live in San Francisco without steady jobs. We were all grifters. Or students.

My heels pierced the dirty carpet. I tromped to Mira's door. Knocked lightly.

"Hey, Stampy," she said.

"Hey, you will have no idea what I did last night." I said. My hands shook slightly as I said, "I got together with Tank."

"You did? Ew!"

"Well, you know. It just happened."

"How was it?"

"I don't know. The Serrano was pretty."

"You did that for a pretty set of sheets?"

"Well...they did have the most lovely French cursive on them, all silky. But, oh, shut up. No."

"Anyway..."

"Anyway, I just wanted to share."

"Oh, I have something to share," Mira said.

"What?"

"I got promoted at Quadra. That boutique on Haight I work at."

"Oh, awesome."

She closed the door.

I moved to the couch. Took off the fuchsia heels I had worn for the past few days. Glanced at the nails emerging in place of taps. Tossed them to the corners of the sunlit room.

A bay window opened onto the bustling intersection. Electrical bus wires stretched in patterned strands from their third floor view. Exhaust plumes. Lurching past hordes of people. Tourists. Residents. Mariachis. Homeless people. Merging and meshing in front of El Noche with the transvestite chanteuses taking smoke breaks on the curb. Leaning against the purple wall with a black owl mural. The club sign's yellow bulbs, spotted. Indigo outlines. Red at the core.

I looked out my window. At the drag queen lounging against the wall. In emerald sparkle slink. She palmed a cigarette off a guy with a messenger bag. Six pack under one arm.

I turned away from the window. Picked up my shoes. Padded to my room. Opened the door. Sat down on the bed. The old duvet with its bursts of orange petunias was bunched and tumbled on the sheets. Stains of ink and menstrual blood. The small room hedged with piles of clothing and magazines. 1960s fabric patterns stretched blue and orange with polka dots along the wall.

I took off my top: a low-slung cowl-neck affixed at the back with a safety pin. Dropped it on the floor. Went to the closet to pull out something new. I felt myself still buzzing with the speed I consumed with Tank. A liquid spiral of pleasure. Webbing through my body. An extra perkiness inducing me to pull up my planner. See when I had to work next. Not until tomorrow.

Exhausted from work, I threw myself on the thin black couch.

Mira emerged from her room. Spread out paper maché and cloth puppets. Covering the coffee table and carpet. She set out tempura paint. A rough horsehair brush. Neglected to throw down any of the loose pages of the SF Weekly that were left on the kitchen table for that purpose.

I glanced up, not saying anything. Mira was messy.

Red paint met a tube sock fragment. Leg to one puppet. I sighed. Watched as a red fleck splotched on the floor.

My cell phone rang. High metallic trill. I sighed again. Fumbled through my purse. Pulled into a half-crouch.

"What the hell." The blotchy orange painting on the wall stared down at me. A starburst of aquamarine with a red target painted on it. Spotlight: attack.

I flipped open my phone.

"It's Angelina! I'm coming back!"

"You are? Oh my God, Fantastic!" While convalescing at her mom's house, Angelina kept in touch with me. Rattling through the phone lines with electrostatic stories of parties gone awry. We exchanged long emails. Lived vicariously through each other's gossip.

"When? How?" I continued.

"Well, I – "

"Who is that?" said Mira from the floor.

"It's Angelina."

"Wow! Let me talk to her!"

"Fine." I passed over the phone.

It was beginning to get dark. I could see the glimmering lights of the bars beginning to blink to life below. Cabs rushed by. Yellow lights. Squealing streaks against the night. A giant martini glass struck up through the haze.

I turned away. Took the phone that Mira offered.

"Okay, when?" I said.

"Next week! Mira said I could stay with you guys. Work on getting a job, then save for my own apartment. I'm so excited!"

I sprawled on the floor. "Okay. If you think you can do it. Are you sure you want to couch surf for that long?"

"It's okay, Billy Vegas said I could stay with him for awhile. We go way back. You know."

"That's true. Okay, no, it's cool with me. We have couches. We have floors and all that. I can't wait to see you."

"Awesome. Okay, I'll see you Thursday!"

I hung up.

Chapter 8 — SAN FRANCISCO 2.0

Angelina careened through the door. Returning to San Francisco after being gone for eight months. Her long limbs emerged from a tight sweater. Q-ball eyes turned on me.

I waited for her at the landing of the Haight place. Green stripes on the walls. Sparse leaf wallpaper.

Angelina was laden down with a backpack and tote bag. Knit cap over two brown braids. Camel boots pulled over her jeans.

I stepped carefully.

"Greyhound okay?" I said.

"They searched my stuff, but they always do that. Oh my God! I'm so happy to see you!"

"Yeah, totally." We embraced. Her bags fell awkwardly against my shoulder. It was late. About one am. Angelina took the bus from the Greyhound station in South of Market. Before that the Greyhound from Phoenix. It was a long haul. Her's was a long journey.

The red-eyed deer tapestry above the kitchen table shone iridescent.

"Do you want a drink? Coffee? Something?" I said. "I don't really have any food."

"Actually, do you want to come to the liquor store for a sec? I need some tin foil." We pulled apart. Angelina set her bag on the floor.

"Yeah, let's do it."

We traipsed down the three staircases to the street. Jabbering rapidly about Mira's latest hi jinx. The dirty cream molding of the stairs folded around us. We descended. Came finally to an iron-scrolled gate. Angelina's shoulders moved in frenetic pace. Un-caged.

The K&H Market sent forth a warm glow under the streetlights. Open door revealing Snickers and Ho-Ho's. Pints of brandy on the back shelves. We went in.

In the small storefront, Angelina was a ball of energy. I could feel the tension inside of her. Moving arms like wires towards the saran wrap. Zip-locks. Aluminum foil. She picked up the yellow box in the fluorescent half-light. Hefted it in one palm.

"This'll do," she said.

When we got back to my room, Angelina pulled out a rectangular slab of foil. Flattened it using a hardback copy of *Nightwood*. She asked me if I had a pen that I didn't want. I gave her one. She reduced it to a tube. Pulled a tiny packet of newspaper out of her pocket. Tossed it on my bed.

"You ready?"

"Sure," I said.

She shook a few grains of speed from the packet onto the foil. Held the aluminum foil in one hand. Put the tube in her mouth. Angelina situated the tube above the foil. Lit the lighter underneath. The speed became liquid. Began to smoke. She took a deep breath. Leaned back against my mattress. Blew sweet smoke into the air.

"Oh God! It's been awhile. I stopped at Jeff's on the way back. I just needed to get some shit. I've been clean for a year and three months, Lena. That long. Fuck it." She drew in another hit.

Angelina relapsed. After a year of sobriety that she left town to get.

"You wanna try?" she said to me.

"Sure." I was down for whatever at this point. Addiction was her battle, as far as I was concerned. I wasn't dealing with my own addiction, yet. I didn't care, at this point, about being Angelina's enabler.

I took the apparatus. Tried to figure out what she so gracefully accomplished.

"No, the other end. Yeah. there. Now light that end. Breath through the tube. Not so close… Ok! Yeah!"

Angelina was back. And so was the party.

I walked down Haight St. to Quadra the next day. Mira asked me to come in. Ostensibly to check out her new window displays. I hoped she could slide me some free merchandise. I was not disappointed.

Mira leaned over the display case. Her voice fluttered.

"Now," she said. "These would be perfect on you." She pulled forth a pair of long blue-feathered chandelier earrings. Slid them across to me. I held them in my hand. Their delicate filaments enchanted. I lifted one onto an ear.

The store was mostly empty. An array of purses lined the walls. Racks upon racks of light sequined tops. Low-cut halters. I didn't see the woman come up behind Mira until she was almost upon her.

"Just what do you think you've been doing? Writing down credit card numbers and thinking you can get away with it!" She grabbed Mira's arm. Wheeled her around.

I turned abruptly. The earrings clenched in my hand. I sidled out of the store. From outside, leaning against the glass just out of sight, I could just hear things go down.

As it sounded, a co-worked had reported Mira for writing down credit card numbers. A number of customers reported fraud on their accounts after shopping at Quadra. All were rung up by Mira.

She came out a few minutes later without her name tag. Clutching a cardboard box. Hairbrush. Hand sanitizer. Walking fast. Her head down. Towards Zona Rosa.

I jogged a little to catch up.

"Are you going to be okay?" I said.

"No, I'm not going to be fucking okay! I just got fucking fired! I needed this job. Those fucking bitches I worked with. They turned me in."

"God, I'm sorry. I stole the earrings, for what it's worth."

She glanced over at the blue feathers. "Well that's good. She'll get a final slap in the face then. Cunt." Mira walked faster and faster. Bent over. Heaved with sobs. I patted her on the back, awkwardly.

"It's just that...like... I always get fired from jobs. I always run scams because they don't pay me enough. It's like, sometimes I get fired for other reasons, but I get fired. I always get fired."

I always got fired too. I worked two real full-time jobs in San Francisco. A nonprofit for the homeless and Devechio & Associates. Filling in between were a million temp gigs from Pathways Personnel. I was always fired, eventually. Mental illness. Queer weirdness. Artistic priorities. Dionysian tendencies.

I am too disabled to sustain a job.

None of us were making much money in 2004. Mira routinely shoplifted food for us.

Angelina returned to San Francisco with the intention of being a model or a stripper. She stayed our couch for several months, reacquainting herself with her old drug habits. She was still without employment, naked or otherwise.

After a long lull in gigs, I started a temp job in industrial Dog Patch. The job required me to wake up at 4:45 am. Catch three different types of public transportation. Commute for an hour and a half in order to work as a receptionist in a roofing company. I took the job. Ran with it.

Things were desperate. It felt good to bring home a rotisserie chicken and a bottle of cheap vodka for Angelina and Mira. The way we were as friends: if one of us had money we bought food and drugs for the others. When I was broke Mira stole for me. When I had a little money coming in from temping, I made sure my friends were able to eat.

Angelina, Mira and I were codependent in a very deep way. Practically keeping each other alive in a fundamentally unsustainable way. Everyone in our desperate world was living off of someone, somehow.

Are we still all living off of each other? Must we? A certain amount of transactional interdependence is how society works. Too much becomes exploitation, a boundary violation, the end of the relationship.

How can I know when it's enough? I never can.

Chapter 9— GRIFTERS

Mira's income came from swiping purses from the clubs we went to. She took credit cards and IDs from the wallets. Used them to siphon money out of accounts. Sometimes she would use the credit cards to buy expensive things. Return them for cash. Other times, gift cards to Sephora. Or hotel rooms for us to party in.

I learned by that point, how to turn my head the other way. I had ethics. I did. Never practiced her practices. Never preached to her against them, either.

The problem was, I was so ground down by lack of money. Loyalty. Addiction to the speed she kept giving me. Now that I could barely afford coke any more. We clung to each other in an increasingly hostile world. I felt I had to tolerate her criminal habits. My friends had flaws. So did I. These same friends were the people keeping me from starving. Keeping me from being alone.

I was afraid to be alone.

Inside, I was alone. As we are all fundamentally alone.

I am alone, always now.

The closeness I sought from Angelina, Mira and Limone was only a panacea to the huge void. *The Well of Loneliness* I felt. Psychiatrically Disabled. Medicated. Socially awkward. Speedy.

I wrote pornography. Stared at MySpace. The gulf separating me from other people. When I did a lot of drugs, I became trapped by my high-ness.

Alone and high at eleven am? It was hard to communicate with other people. Who were instead at jobs. Drinking coffee. Reading the New York Times. Having brunch.

When I took the roofing receptionist job, I was more engaged with the outside, waking world. For a brief time.

Mira bought a bunch of E at a steep discount, to resell. There was a pricking at the back of my neck that some of it would trickle down to me. I was an opportunist when it came to drugs. In that, Angelina and Mira and I had quite a bit in common. There were reasons why we were friends.

Another night. Angelina and I sat cross-legged on the floor of my room. Picked at the carpet. She still did not have a job. We were broke. We wanted drugs. It was about three am.

"Hey, do you think Mira is asleep?"

"I don't know, why?" I said.

"I was just thinking..."

"What were you thinking..."

"You know how she has that E?"

"Oh."

Complicit, I watched. Angelina got up. Stealthily padded out of the room. She came back a few moments later with a tense smile on her face and a clenched fist.

"Oh my god! You did it!"

She opened her fist to reveal two octagonal pills. Passed one to me.

"Thank you!"

The E came on slowly then suddenly. I watched Angelina. Hoped she'd be induced to touch me. She was not. I felt the welling. Waves of desire. Urge to express it. I touched her arm where she lay on the bed.

"No, oh no, Lena. Come on. You know I'm not like that."

"Oh, ok. Sorry." I retreated back to my corner of the sheets. Felt the spiraling warmth with no outlet. It seemed a waste.

Tank poured me whiskey into the flask in my kitchen the following night.

"Come on," he said. "Let's take the bus to the Serrano Hotel. The 26 works." The kitchen was a tight hallway. Hung with Korean film posters and plastic lemons.

I leaned against the wall with one hand on the table. Watching my chipped, irregular nails. I was a biter. The cracked linoleum peeled beneath the kitchen table.

"To the Serrano?" I asked. "So you're still staying there still?"

"It'll be fun. You'll be with me."

We ran outside into the freezing rain. The drops jetted through my black lace scarf. Ran down my cheeks. Dripped off of my nose. The Haight was full of homeless kids. Lurching toothless men with half-pints of brandy in paper bags, like him. Pitted concrete stretched past the shuttered vintage shops.

"Come on," I said, half-heartedly looking upwards. "Let's take a cab. I have eight dollars."

"Whiskey! Rain! Romance! It's so Tom Waits. It's brilliant. It has to be the bus. Tom Waits would not take a cab." He lifted both hands to the sky. Drops from the Happy Donut awning hit his bald head. The dark expanse of Haight Street stretched in front of us. Seethed to the yellow glare of the Pollo Asada sign. Scarlet cursive on urine.

"You're ridiculous," I said

"I'm alive."

"I'm alive too, and I'm cold."

"How about the BART?" he said.

"They won't let you take the flask."

"They don't have to see the flask." He cocked an eyebrow, bristly.

"Whatever," I sniffed. My hand shot up as soon as the Radio Cab shot by. It came to an abrupt halt in front of a Guardian kiosk. I gave him a hard look. Dragged him into the back seat.

"Shut it and let me talk.," I whispered to Tank. "I learned this from Mira." I fell back into the soft, nubby upholstery. Whimpered, "Oh, it's so cold! We're only just going to our hotel? I only have eight dollars but can you please take us there?"

The young man looked back from the front seat. The streetlight illuminated the sparks of rain as they sluiced beneath his wipers. Beneath the thin brown stubble he was East Indian. Sincere.

He smiled. "I will take you."

Tank looked blindsided. I smiled.

Whispered, "I love being a girl. There's nothing cuter than a lost young couple." I gave him the address. Cuddled into the backseat. We crested up Valencia. The rows of palms crescendoed past performance spaces. Burnt-out storefronts. The odd Thai restaurant. I suddenly felt like I had things figured out.

I was naked under French-scrawled sheets in Tank's room in the Serrano. Curled up. Breathing heavy with sleep. The gold framed mirror reflected nothing but the silver morning outside. The hotel room was still. No bodies in flight. Tank was next to me. Shirt on. Drooling into the crook of his hand. His eyelid fluttered when a bang came from the door. He jerked awake.

Tank muttered, "Stay here," to me. He pulled on his pants. Fumbled with the door. Pushed back the three chain locks. I peeked from my hidden perch under the blanket.

Tank opened the door to the huge, bearded man from the other night. Another man that I didn't recognize. I froze. Barely awake. Completely covered. Pinned. Listening.

The two sketchy men sat down on the other side of the bed. Began smoking meth with Tank. It was about eleven in the morning.

"Do you have 'em?"

"Yeah, here." Tank passed another bundle of checks over to the bearded man and an envelope to his companion. He drew deeply on the pipe. Let out a haze of cloying smoke.

I kept peeking throughout the hour. Prayed they wouldn't discover me. Wondering what would happen. I closed my eyes tightly. Wished to escape into the dark abscess of my mind. Knew, as I heard the coughs and laughter, that they were still here.

I was trapped. Nude. In a hotel room. Illegally procured. With unknown criminals. Smoking meth.

My thoughts crystallized in that moment. The glow of the morning became brighter. The voices became louder. I heard laughter. The hiss of the pipe.

When they finally rose to leave, I had shut down everything but breathing. I waited, clenched, until the door was triple chain-locked again.

Tank walked back to the bed.

"Here, let me have a hit first," I said coldly. I don't think I'm awake yet."

Chapter 10 — LOS ANGELES VIA ECHO PARK

The afterparty swirled around us. Three am. Billy Vegas, Angelina and Ben and I stood in the corner of a stranger's kitchen. Drank from Ben's flask. Talked about going to Los Angeles for a spur-of-the-moment road trip the next day.

"I'm actually a native, but you wouldn't know it," I said. Wiped powder off my nose. "I was born in Glendale, but we left when I was three."

"I always though Glendale was like an idyllic farm town in central California," said Angelina.

"No, it's right in the middle of Los Angeles. I don't know much about it, except I rode my tricycle into the pool at one point. The pool was at my parents house in Century City. West of Glendale. LA's big. Super-big. Way bigger than San Francisco."

"Well, perhaps we can find a pool for you to fall into. There's shitloads apparently. I have this converted van that's like an RV now. It'll sleep five. If we bring Mira that's all of you. We won't have to pay for places to sleep. It won't cost that much. You'd be surprised, Los Angeles is so much cheaper than San Francisco. They have these taco trucks everywhere."

Ben was the ringleader of this expedition. I had faith in him. In his thirties, he was the most reliable adult out of all of us. If Ben said it would be okay, it would be okay.

I took a gulp of his vodka. Looked across the room at the bright colors against the wall. People moving apart in new combinations. A spur-of the moment trip to LA might work out for me right now. Things with Tank were getting hot in a bad way.

The next morning Ben pulled up at our apartment. Double-parked. I struggled to wake Angelina. Mira had been up all night packing. Making puppets. Possibly also rewiring the stereo but I had dropped off for a while and wasn't sure.

Angelina's hands looked like white gloves daintily slicking out from the blanket. She slept on the floor of my small room. She slept on my floor and Mira's floor alternately depending on who she was getting along with best that day. Her situation was precarious but she seems to be coping. She was a hustler.

Mira came busting through my door with rhythm sticks Banged them together. I hadn't seen those since I was in kindergarten. I couldn't help laughing as she danced around the room stroking grooved stick to straight stick

"Get up bitches!" Mira sang loudly.

We managed to pull our bags downstairs after six missed calls from Ben. I looked at my flip phone finally. Saw a text that read, "WTF you guys? I'm getting a crepe."

The van had seventies wood panels. Orange flowered curtains. We sat around a built in table in the middle section. Ben drove. Mira rode shotgun. She twisted around periodically to shoot an imaginary gun at us.

"Pew, pew!" Mira yelled.

Billy Vegas pulled out a bag of coke in the back.

"Let's throw down what we've got," he said. "It's gonna be a long ride."

I smiled. Jolted along with my hands on the beige plastic of the table. I reached into my clutch. Pulled out the baggie from last night with a thin line of powder still evident.

"I've got a little. I might have more in my stuff but I want to save that for when we go out."

I reached back and pulled closed the back curtains. The side curtains. It was dark in the van as we motored towards Los Angeles from San Francisco. Closed in. The wood-grain cabinets. The stink of the toilet we were all afraid to use.

Angelina batted her eyelashes at Billy.

Billy emptied a small pile of coke onto the tabletop. Gestured at me. I poured mine out into his. He began to cut lines. He offered the first to Angelina. The second to me.

Pulling his face up from the table, he said, "So what do you girls do that makes you happy, that like gets you really going?"

"I'm a writer." I said, "I'm working on a book right now. I'll be all alone in my room and typing something and then be like "I'm a genius, I love what I just wrote." It makes me really happy."

"What about, you, Angel?"

"Well, I don't think I'm a genius ever. I don't know, I get excited about dressing up…. Going out… Like, the time in the afterparty when no one gives a shit and everyone's high. I'm really excited to be back in San Francisco. Getting sober sucked."

"Oh God! I bet. Did you have to do, like NA and stuff?"

"Yeah, I did. I couldn't talk to anyone for a long time, I couldn't contact Lena or Mira. That hurt so bad to be away from my friends. As soon as I came back I was just like, fuck it, time for me. Time to take care of me. And then I smoked a bunch of speed. I was getting fat, too, it was really essential that I smoke a bunch of speed before I saw anyone so I wouldn't be humiliated."

"I know what you mean," I said, "I would totally choose being a drug addict over being fat any day. Absolutely." We high-fived.

"Well, you look beautiful," Billy said to Angelina. A slender drug addict. He laid out more lines.

Ben, his curly fro visible over the headrest, said, "Are you guys doing lines back there?

"Share! Share! Share! Share!" went Mira.

"It's not speed," said Angelina.

"Don't share. Don't care." She responded, flipping her head in the breeze from the window. Her hair was wild. "I want to blast the radio and stick my head out the window like a dog!"

"I'll have a bump," said Ben.

I looked at the others. Worried that police would see us.

 "Are you sure there aren't any cops?"

"Lena, you are such a fucking pussy." said Angelina. She took a key-bump from the pile. Walked the couple steps to Ben's captain's chair. He leaned around. She put it to his nose while he drove.

"Ah, yeah." He said. Angelina sat down with a smirk on her face.

When Ben finally stopped driving I could hear the ocean barking against the rocks. My legs were stiff. My mind ran fast. There were little whorls of color at the edge of my senses. My nose felt cold. Cleaned out.

Mira braided the armrest fringe for a few hours. We were out of coke. I was dying to go outside.

Ben swiveled around to look at us. Me with shoulders tight. Hunched over the table. Picking at what was not there. Angelina and Billy talking deep into each other's eyes.

"You guys? Do you want to go outside? See the beach? We've been on the 101 for a while now. I think we're going to stop and spend the night here. So come on out before it gets too dark. You guys look like you need a little reset."

"Oh, hells to the yeah." I cracked my neck. Bent it back. Got up from the built-in bench.

Angelina finished a final point she was making to Billy. Looked up. Her eyes followed the door as I pulled it open to reveal the sky an eerie shade of pale. The ocean roared below us.

We were on the cliffs. Chocolate brown rock dusted with sand met my bare foot as I stepped out. Felt solid ground again after so much lurching. Spouts of water came up as waves dashed against the rock. I could smell salt and something deeper. A dank, fishy odor. Something like rotten seaweed.

I looked back. Angelina and Billy held hands. Stared at the low sun with its pink streaks thrown against the horizon. Ben smoked a cigarette. I couldn't see Mira. She emerged from behind the van. Ran in circles. Tried to catch something I couldn't see.

"Yeah. I could definitely sleep here tonight," Billy said. "You guys want to sleep, like, actually on the cliffs?

We can't." Ben said. "Coast Guard says no camping. We can park here. If I draw the curtains and we're all inside we can get away with it, but we can't sleep outside."

"Damn. The air's so fresh out here. In there it smells like..."

"Like Lena's farts." Mira said.

"Everybody poops," I said.

"Well you didn't have to take that dump that we've been smelling for the past four hours. Like, WTF was that?" Angelina held a delicate hand to her nose.

"I'm so sorry, you guys. Really. There was nowhere to stop. Coke makes me have to shit."

"Well, if you've got to drop a deuce somewhere, you've got to just be unapologetically awesome about it." Billy said. "I drop a deuce whenever I go into a new person's house. It's like I'm leaving my calling card. I'm claiming the space. 'Billy was here.' People think it's funny. Like it's my shtick."

"Somehow I think that would be even less acceptable coming from a girl." I said.

"Yeah. I mean, can you imagine if one of us tried that? That would so not be cool," Angelina said.

We spread out along the rocks.

That night in the van I curled up on a makeshift bunk. My feet bumped into Mira.

"What the fuck!" She yowled. "Stay on your own goddamn side."

"Hey. Hey. Just trying to sleep."

"We're all just trying to sleep. Can you two shut up," said Angelina from a bunk opposite. The table and bench had turned over to reveal a small bed. Bunks pulled out from the sides. There was a loft in the back that Ben slept on. I could hear the waves crashing. Coming for us.

It was so dark in there. Still I was racing. Awake. I could feel Mira tugging on the blanket. Shifting around in the blackness. I wished I had more coke. I wished it was morning.

Finally, I could see dawn through the edges of the curtains. A blue glow faded in with the smell of salt.

I slept then, fitfully. Finally.

Ben and Billy were not getting along. Ben insisted on driving the whole way, which was fine with me. I didn't want to drive.

Ben drove down the 101. He and Billy were clearly butting heads on who was the alpha male of the group. I hung back. This was not my battle.

The night I met Billy, I gave him a blowjob at the Phoenix Hotel. My body doesn't lay claim. My mind does, and theirs. You could say heart, but I hate to use that word so colloquially.

I watched Angelina make out with Billy in the back of the van. Aroused. Conflicted. Attributed the wetness between my thighs to the speed that Mira threw down.Not able to face up to my queerness yet.

We bumped over freeways down to Echo Park. I only heard of Echo Park in that movie *Mi Vida Loca*. I was excited to see if it still had that gangster glamour. Otherness excited me.

I become the other. I perform the other. I am inside and outside.

In Echo Park, we watched the palm trees and the little stucco houses with bars on the windows. The murals on the stairs leading up the cliffs. The lake with its huge blue expanse. Lotuses. Birds. So many birds. A spout of water came out from the middle of the lake. The sun came through it. Dazzling. I pressed my face to the window.

"They have nature here! Like, in the city! We don't have this in San Francisco."

"I know, right? This is like kind of ghetto but they still have this beautiful lake that everyone can hang out in." Ben said.

I watched women running laps around the pool. Marching slowly with children. Couples picnicking on the grass. Men with metal detectors followed men with dogs. A fenced off island that looked almost primordial.

I wanted to live here in Echo Park one day after so long in a concrete box in San Francisco. My small room with its windows to bars. Restaurants. Sidewalks. Airshafts to other windows. My small room felt oppressive. I wanted to see the sky. I saw yellow lines down the asphalt only. Never seagulls rising in flight. I wanted to see the water. I watched a pelican dive for fish.

"When do we get to move here, Angelina?" I said.

"When I make it big as a model."

"Well Foxy Jennifer did, actually. " Ben said. "By shakin' her ass at the Spearmint Rhino. She moved down here. That's who we're going to visit. She's an old girlfriend of mine and I think she might let us stay with her."

"What about sleeping in the van?" Billy said.

"You saw how much that sucked." Mira threw in from the back seat.

We pulled up to a pink stucco house.

Ben said, "Let me just go in for a little bit. I will come out and get you guys once I know it's ok." He left us there.

At this point we were dirty. Filthy dirty. Me and Angelina smeared makeup on our faces to look presentable for this girl. Foxy Jennifer, Angelina informed me, was a friend of hers who used to dance at the Golden Horseshoe. Had given her some good girl advice in the past.

"I think I could be a stripper," Angelina said. "I really do. I'm totally going to try out at the Lusty Lady once we get back in town."

"Awesome," I said.

"You guys look like the Manson family," Foxy Jennifer said. She peered into the van. "I'm having a shitty day today. I'm sick, like I can't really handle having guests. Why don't you guys just pull this van over to the Walgreens parking lot on Sunset and sleep there tonight. There's a taco truck. You'll be set."

She leaned back against the chain link fence. Her long hair black whipped in the breeze. Her aquiline face was stern. Black eyeliner. Gold lip-gloss.

"Please, Foxy Jennifer? Please!" said Angelina, leaning out the door.

"Oh, I wish I could just take just you."

"But what about me," Ben said.

"You're like orphan kittens, seriously. I can't do this. My place is really small and I'm trying to get clean. Do you know anyone else here?"

"I might know someone!" Billy to the rescue. He sat in the back of the van.

"You're always trying to one-up me, it's not cool." Ben said. In his voice were the first flashes of anger.

"Well, I do know people. Paradise Boys play in LA all the time. I've got peeps. Stick with me."

Ben looked crushed.

"Why don't you guys work this out. I've got some laundry I need to deal with. It was nice seeing you, Ben. Call me sometime. Okay, later." Foxy Jennifer loped away. Her long legs in platform wedges moving fast.

Not her problem. A group of impoverished drug addicts. Looking for shelter.

What we wanted? She couldn't give. It is important not to ask for too much. Not to need too much. I struggle with this. Boundaries. Addiction. To different kinds of validations. Transactions. I give a story. I take the eye's time.

Chapter 11 — SWEET CAROLINE'S

Ben opened the driver's side door. Sat down. He put his head in his hands. Brown curls fell down. I felt a twinge of sympathy.

Billy kept talking. "If you'd only listened to me," he said. "We could be staying with Caroline in her sweet pad in Los Feliz. But no. You insisted we go up to Echo Park. Look how rockin' this ended up."

Ben's lips were tight. He revved the engine. Started driving. Fast. Curved around winding roads down to Sunset.

We sped down Sunset Blvd until Billy said, "What the hell are you doing, Ben? Do you have any idea where you're going?"

"Why do you constantly question my authority?"

"Why do you think you're fucking in charge?"

"This is my van. The trip was my idea. These are my friends."

"These are my girls. My friends."

"Well look." Ben pulled off on a side street next to a boarded up Fallas Paredes. "You can all get out now. The taxi ride is over. Follow your fucking alpha prince, because obviously I'm just the chauffeur. I am sick of being fucking used. Get out, all of you. Get your stuff and get out."

He opened the van doors. Began pulling our luggage into the street. Angelina and I looked at each other. Bewildered.

"Even me? Mira said.

"Even you."

We jumped out. I sat on my suitcase on a strange street in Hollywood. Watched Ben close the doors. Get back inside the van.

"Look man, you know you look like such the asshole right now. I'm going to tell everyone in San Francisco that you dropped three ladies off on the side of the road in Hollywood."

"This doesn't look like Hollywood." I said.

"Do you even know what Hollywood looks like?" Angelina said.

"No, not especially. I just didn't think there'll be a Game Stop and a Jamba Juice. Where are all the stars?"

"You naive little fuckers can find your own way now, I am done. Done!" Ben yelled out the window as he pulled away. I watched the orange van drive away.

Would it always be so tragic? Would I always be so tragic? Was there any hope? Was it all worth it? Attention is validating.

The transactional nature of fandom and friendship. The same and different. We all make our choices. I made mine.

Mira, Angelina, Billy and I sat on the sidewalk in Hollywood in 2004. Stunned for a few minutes. Billy fumbled in his pocket. Turned to Angelina.

"Do you have a cigarette?" Billy asked.

"No. I'm out."

I felt the sun beat down on my shoulders. I wore a T-shirt that said "High on Aerobics" on the back. My friend Molly the stripper sold it to me in a yard sale in Portland. Mira slapped me on the back.

"What are we gonna do now?" Mira said.

"Don't panic, ladies." Billy said. "Don't panic. I know a girl called Caroline who said I could always stay with her when I was in LA. Don't worry Angelina, she's just a friend. She's really a doll. You guys will love her. Does anybody have a phone?"

I pulled out my cell. Now that Ben was gone, Angelina and I were the only two people with cell phones. Mira never had a cell phone. She preferred to make her calls on other people's phones. She didn't have the funds or desire to be saddled with a cell phone plan. Tank didn't have a cell phone, either. It made him extremely hard to get ahold of. Either he was with me or he wasn't anywhere to be found. Phantom calls came in at night from unknown destinations.

Billy didn't have a cell phone either. Some people didn't have the money. Some people either didn't have jobs or parents with money to cover a family plan.

"Let me make a few calls," Billy said.

At SquaresVille, a vintage shop in Los Feliz. Billy's friend led us past the cash register between two racks of macramé swimwear. Her name was Caroline. She was almost a little too rotting peach nice. I was suspect. Drug-addled paranoia was too often my practice.

"Now this is my shop. I'm the manager. No one's in today." She lowered her voice conspiratorially. "Why don't each of you pick out one piece of clothing and we'll just pretend it never happened." Caroline giggled, awash in her own generosity. I liked her a lot more now.

I walked around between racks of eighties dresses and seventies shirts. Finally, I found the perfect thing. A cotton dress with alternating black and white diagonal stripes in panels across the bust. Black and white diagonals were a thing for me. It was low cut, too. Again a thing I preferred. I tried it on. It was perfect summer loungewear.

"Is this...okay?" I asked Caroline.

"Of course! Let me put it in a bag for you."

I liked Caroline now.

Caroline's place was a top floor apartment. She sublet it with her boyfriend. Sweeping windows opened upon green lawns. The wide stretch of Los Feliz Blvd. Cars lurched across through the windows. Inside was central air conditioning. Plenty of space.

"There's something about Los Angeles that's so different from San Francisco," I said.

"Yeah," Billy said, "Without a car we were assed out. There was no way we were getting anywhere until the pretty lady picked us up."

"And then there's so many more green spaces. Normal people can have large beautiful apartments. There isn't that tiny cramped feeling." Angelina said, "I can see why Ben wants to move here."

"Ben has been sick of San Francisco for awhile," said Mira. "I mean, closing up Audiophoria was the first step to getting the hell out. I predict he'll move here."

We killed time in Caroline's apartment.

"Where's your friend, Ben?" said Caroline.

"He's the guy that dropped us on the sidewalk," Billy said. "I imagine he might be with Foxy Jennifer, but don't know exactly."

"He has friends here." Mira butted in. "He knows people. But he wanted to know Foxy Jennifer a little better."

"In the biblical sense." Billy said. Angelina laughed.

"Well my god, you guys must be so dusty and tired. Does anyone want a bath? There's whirlpool jets in there." Angelina and Billy's eyes met.

Mira and I ate ice cream with Caroline while trying not to listen to the sex sounds coming out of the bathroom. It went on until the pint of white chocolate raspberry truffle Häagen Dazs was gone. We were reduced to talking about working retail. How to deal with backstabbing co-workers.

"If someone's really got in in for me, I just cut their hours bit by bit until they quit." Caroline said. "It's sort of a passive-aggressive way of firing them. Then was don't have to give them unemployment or anything."

"Oh, that's excellent," said Mira. "Do you think I could get unemployment? I was fired."

"What for? If you don't mind me asking?"

"Well, giving stuff to people. Stealing I guess."

"Oh, that's no big deal. But wait, how long did you work there?"

"Two months."

"No, you need to have worked somewhere between three and nine months, preferably nine months and up to get unemployment."

"Diarrhea-balls."

We followed Caroline to a party in Silver Lake. Through the windows of her car at night Los Angeles seemed like San Francisco in a way. We passed though winding tiny streets in the Silver Lake Hills. So many street that I got lost again. I had no idea where I was when we got out of her car. We walked into a costume party where everyone seemed to be in their underwear.

"I didn't know that this was this kind of party," I said in Angelina's ear.

"Oh come on." Angelina said. "Would you really want to be in your underwear right now? I think we look better as we are." Girls in marabou and hot pants swirled past my shoulders. A drink jostled onto Mira's short blonde head. Red punch dripped down. She elbowed frantically.

I moved through the crowd looking for alcohol. I had a little bit of coke left, but I wanted to save it for when I really needed it. When it could be better used by sharing. Preferably with someone I wanted to sleep with. I looked for a possible seduction target.

I stumbled into Ben and Foxy Jennifer. They refilled red plastic cups at the kitchen counter. The high ceiling looked blue. Ben and Foxy Jennifer looked cozy. I sidled in aware I couldn't get a drink if I didn't talk to them. Not sure how this interaction would turn out.

"Hi, you guys."

"Oh! Hi Lena." Ben said, "You got the rest of the family with you?"

"They're somewhere around here."

Foxy Jennifer barely looked up. She was stirring something blue that looked like Blue Curacao into her drink.

"I... I wanted to apologize for Billy. He really was out of line in acting like that."

"Yes. Yes. He was."

"I don't know. I mean, like maybe you guys could talk? Work it out? We'd really like to travel with you again."

Foxy Jennifer looked up from her cup. "I think what she's trying to say is that both of you were assholes and you've screwed her out of a roof over her head." She looked at me finally. Amber eyes in a tan face. Kohl-rimmed eyes.

I met her gaze for a moment. Ducked to pour some vodka into my glass. Popov. That was about how I felt. I didn't feel like I could reach for the Blue Curacao, directly below Foxy Jennifer's imposing breasts. I didn't feel like I deserved to. I crept away. Clutched my vodka and vodka. How dare I go in for mixers? I got about six feet away from the table when Ben tugged my elbow.

"Lena."

"Ben! Hey!"

"Listen, I've been doing a lot of thinking. I feel really bad about how I treated you girls. I mean, what happened between me and Billy was one thing. That's a different issue. But to dump you and Angel and Mira out on the street like that was not okay. Like anything could happen out there. Have you guys been alright?"

"Yeah, luckily Billy knew this really nice girl. We've been okay. It still feels precarious, though. Staying with a total stranger."

"Maybe you guys can come back with me tonight. Sleep in the van outside of Foxy Jennifer's if you'd feel more comfortable. Then we can head back tomorrow, or the day after tomorrow. I hear there's a pool party at the Standard tomorrow night that might be pretty great."

"Oh, that does sound fun. Thank you. Let me talk to the others." I squeezed him on the shoulder. Moved off into the crowd.

I bumped shoulder to shoulder with Angelina and Mira. Filled them in.

"How do we know they won't fight again?" Angelina gestured at Billy Vegas's waistcoat. He was on the couch earnestly talking about the guitar solo in a Small Faces song.

"I don't think we can know. I think we can just hope." I said. Took a drink. The plastic bumped my sore nose. "At least we know he's differentiated between his anger at him and his anger at us. Like he sees us as different people."

"Thank God for that. Sure, I'll spend the night in the van tonight. We can get our stuff from Caroline's tomorrow. Billy will follow me, I think." Angelina smiled.

I moved out into the crowd again. Sipped my vodka and vodka. Noticed my old San Francisco hook-up Ian leaning against the door. Watching me with bright, black eyes. Bingo.

Angelina and Billy sat on the curb looking wrecked. Laughed. I got out of Ian's Town Car. Sauntered up to them. My makeup was smeared. My low-cut cowl-neck top below tit. Floppy side boob. I didn't wear bras. Fashion trash.

I sat down next to Angelina. Billy passed me a forty.

"Did you get laid?"

"Hells to the yeah. I got laid."

Angelina dissolves in peals of laughter. "Oh she totally did, I knew it as soon as I saw that guy. That's totally her type." She looked up at me through brown lashes. No mascara. No makeup for perhaps the first time I'd seen her. Freckles shone on her pale cheeks. The blue foil tube top she wore stained with wine.

Sun sifted through the trees above us onto Billy Vegas. He gulped the forty. Screwed a cigarette butt into ash with his booted heel. Kicked a foot out along the asphalt.

"That's how we roll if we're going to be traveller trash. Manson Family trash."

"Yeah," Angelina said. "Did you hear Foxy Jennifer said when she stuck her head in the van? She said we looked like the Manson family in here."

"If I'm around Mira much longer...." I said. "Where is she, anyway?"

"Inside. Sleeping it off. That girl travels with so much go-fast. I don't even fucking know."

"Hey, well you're totally Sharon Tate, anyway," Billy said to Angelina. Stroked a runaway strand of her hair.

"Oh come on," she said. Resisting, but not really.

"Will someone buy me a burger? We can share it," Billy said, gesturing at the Fatburger across the parking lot.

"I'm so broke." Angelina said.

"I can. I guess." I said. We walked across the steaming asphalt towards the yellow and red building.

I tried to never eat fast food. When traveling all bets were off. We were broke. We were hungry. I still had some money on my debit card left over from my past temp jobs. I was willing to spot Billy.

We sat on the yellow stools. I went up and ordered an eight oz. King Burger. He sliced it in half with a plastic knife. We sat there. Meditatively. Munching on a part of old Americana. The first solid food I'd had in a few days. My stomach acids attacked the meat.

I wiped ketchup off my lips. Looked at Billy. A blissful expression on his face.

"Food. Keeps a man alive. You girls and your drunkorexia business. A man's got to eat. Thank you. I won't forget this."

I smiled. "You owe me $2.75."

"Put it on my tab. I'll pay you back all of it when we get back to San Francisco.

Friends ran tabs with other friends. For drug or food money. Depending on who had money at the moment. The way it used to be.

Chapter 12 — HOMEWARD BOUND

I climbing out of the water at the hotel pool party. The buildings around the Standard Hotel reflecting in the pool. Huge billboards around us. Faces reflected in the water.

As I climbed out, Mira tackled me. I floated. Floated on my back in the warm water. The bar next to the pool bright with ivy. Angelina reclined in a white bikini next to the diving board. Night. There was so much light given off by the heat lamps. The pool. The people moving around drinking gin that glowed blue and vodka that glowed yellow. I lay on my back in the water. Backstroke side paddling. I could see a few stars above me, but only a few. These were the only stars of any variety I would see on this trip.

Floating in the water. Bright reflections of huge faces. Tiny lights in windows going up on skyscrapers. We were leaving tomorrow. I was and was not ready. I knew traveling was not sustainable. My life back in San Francisco with it's seedy eking along seemed so distant. I just wanted to float forever on this many colored water. I knew I could not.

Ben drove Mira, Angelina, Billy and I back to San Francisco. We listened to *Leaving on a Jet Plane* by Peter Paul and Mary. Windows open. Night outside. Lights passing fast.

"Oh here," Ben said. "You guys are going to dig this." I pulled out of half sleep to see he was going down a freeway off ramp. Left. Right. He pulled up to an ornate pink sign reading: "The Madonna Inn."

"Oh, I've heard of this place," said Angelina. "You can't be meaning we're staying here? Isn't it like super-expensive?

"No, no. I just figured we could explore a little bit. It's really cool and kitschy. Fun to look at."

He pulled up through the parking lot. Past a rock-walled country cottage main building. A lake with rainbow lights. We went in further. Parked next to a long building laced with white railings that seemed more Swiss Miss than hotel circle.

Angelina stood up. "I'm going to go see if any of those rooms are unlocked."

"Yeah, let's go!" said Mira.

They got out. I stood idly next to the van taking in the warm San Luis Obispo night. I could see that some doors were open. I wasn't sure if it was maid service or hotel guests taking the air. I didn't really feel comfortable investigating.

Billy sat. Smoked on a wheel-well. He got up. Took off in another direction. I watched him go.

The air was damp. It seemed to hold some portent inside the candy-colored lights.

A few minutes later, Angelina came back with something under her jacket.

"We should go, you guys. We should go, now."

We all understood that, implicitly. Got in the van.

A few miles down the freeway, she pulled an intricate, iridescent pink goblet out from under her shirt. It was about ten inches high. Could fit half a bottle of wine so it looked.

"That's gorgeous! Did you steal that?" I said.

"Sure did," Angelina beamed,

"Nice!" Said Billy.

Coming home from Los Angeles and the Madonna Inn, nothing seemed to hold the same sparkle that traveling had. I walked the long avenues from the bus stop to my new temp job in the Sunset. The fog clenched down on me. The routine of maintaining dual personalities wore thin.

I tried to get ahold of Tank. His, "I'm so free without a cell phone, I'm even more free without a stable address," bit was incomprehensibly frustrating. I hadn't seen him in a few weeks. I felt like I had to rely on ESP to get him to call me.

I tried halfheartedly ringing up a few of the hotels Tank stayed in. He checked out of all of them. I ran out of fake names to try.

I wrote in my maudlin diary one morning. Tank called.

"Lena?"

"Tank? I was beginning to think you'd died."

"Naw, I just got busy for awhile. You wanna hang out?"

"Yeah, totally, come over."

When he came up the stairs, I was plucking my eyebrows. Waxing, a habit I would so like to become accustomed to, was too expensive for my current situation. I smeared on a coat of lip-gloss. Turned away from the mirror.

Tank smiled sheepishly. His baldness shiny. His grin missing a tooth. A laptop under his arm.

"Hey, it's good to see you."

"You too. It's been awhile."

"I was in LA. It was crazy. Picture Mira, Angelina, and then this guy Ben. He's usually really cool and stable, but he fought with Billy and dropped us all by the side of the road for awhile. Bunch of total tweakers trying to fend for ourselves."

"Sounds like a party."

"It was and then it wasn't. Hey, do you want to go get brunch? We could go to Squat and Gobble?"

He halfheartedly tucked the tail of his shirt into his pants. "No, I can't. Pretty young girl and old man pervert having breakfast? It's no good. It doesn't look good. I'm going to be getting all these dirty looks from people. Let's just stay inside. I brought my computer. Have you ever played World of Warcraft?

"No. I don't really play computer games."

"Well, I brought my pipe, too." He took a glass tube with a globe on the end from his pocket. "I'm pretty sure there's some speed in here if you want to light it up."

"Oh, thanks." I lay on the bed. Chased the clear liquid methamphetamine around the pipe with a lighter. Waited until the globe filled with smoke. Inhaled. Soon I felt warm and sultry. Tank sat on the bed with me. Intent upon the computer screen.

I passed him the pipe. He took a hit. Passed it back.

"What are you trying to do, there?" I asked.

"It's like, all these people from around the world are playing this computer game. I'm playing with them. It's all live action right now. My team needs me right now to help defeat these Orcs and this wizard."

I took another hit. "So you can't come make a girl happy?"

"I really can't, Lena. These people are depending on me to help with this scrimmage. I can't put the game on hold.

"Okay." I began to do kegels. Bitterly.

My attraction for Tank was difficult to explain. There was something about his ugliness that made me feel like the prettiest little minx when next to him. I felt superior to him, when I didn't feel better than anyone else. There was something about his kindness, his vulnerability, that I liked.

I knew I couldn't take Tank to The Rosetta Bar with me. I didn't care. Drifted away from the clubs.

Tank was a winner out of my past homeless criminal boyfriend. At least he was nice to me. Instead of slapping me around.

I didn't feel like I could demand the top shelf in anything. Tank gave me drugs. He was a generous lover. We never had full-on sex. He went soft as soon as he put it in a condom.

Tank didn't ask more of me than I could give. That was enough.

Reciprocity. Only taking what another is willing to give.

I was content. Until he felt sleazy and dangerous.

As this book may already. Mutual exploitation welds us. I can't make this shit up.

Tank finished his scrimmage with the online Orcs. He suggested we go downtown to the Westin. Jeff was staying there. He had to hand over some fake IDs.

"The St. Francis? That fancy one on the hill? Big crazy beaux-arts thing?"

"No. They wouldn't take the credit card number Jeff had. We figured the one on Market Street would be more low-key. And they were fine about it. He's got a suite. It's like a nonstop party over there. It's hot, though. Real hot. We've got to just get in and get out."

"Ok. I'm ready. I've got my crime knickers on."

We walked briskly through the St Francis lobby. Black and yellow marble made concentric diamonds around huge flower arrangements. The lights were low and recessed. Glossy wood columns encircled them.

At the elevator, I turned to him, "Do we look suspicious?"

"Don't ask, just do. Face forward. Eyes clear."

I faced Tank across the blonde marble elevator. "Where did you lose that tooth, anyway?"

"It was a vulva accident."

"Oh dear God."

"Oh dear God. That is amazing is what you should say. It was amazing. I was like giving this chick head and she was bucking so much she cracked out my tooth.

The elevator opened. We walked down the hall to room #867.

In the hotel room, five men sat around watching porn. Jeff and them yelled things at the screen. Clothed, not masturbating.

I walked in with Tank. Felt the sexual tension in the room. Another guy and girl sat on a hotel room bed. Talking, as the guy turned a glass vial over and over in his hands. I sat next to them.

Tank approached Jeff. Began bargaining.

I was used to being benched. Figured it was time for small talk. I was high, making it easier.

"Hi, I'm Lena."

"Hey girl. I'm Jason."

The other girl smiled. Crossed her legs.

"You two a couple?" Jason gestured at Tank

"Yeah, you could say that."

"That's cool."

We chatted about this and that for a while. I watched Tank and Jeff bicker about payment.

"Hey, do you girls want some molly?" Jason said.

"Ooh, sure." He poured a tablet into my waiting hand. Gave one to the other girl. "Actually, can I have two?" I said.

His face lit up like he was going to get laid for sure. He gave me another pill. I smiled indulgently.

Just then, Tank came to find me. He put his hand on my shoulder.

"We should bail."

"Great meeting you guys. I've got to go. Thanks for everything," I said. Sincerely as I could. Followed Tank out into the hall. Two pills of E for us in my purse. Win.

Chapter 13 — SHIT HITS THE FAN

Angelina took a huge hit off the speed pipe. Left to audition at the Lusty Lady. She pulled on her boots and was gone.

When Angelina came back, she was demoralized. She thumped down on the two mattresses in Mira's room. Hit the pipe again.

"It's like… It's like… I just danced totally naked for strangers. They told me I wasn't good enough."

"Oh shit. I'm sorry."

"Yeah. You wouldn't understand. You haven't done this kind of sex work yet, Miss College Education. Only your porn writing. That's not like real naked sex work like I just had to do."

I knew she was right.

"So what happened," I said.

"I showed up. Talked to the guy. Then I changed into my outfit. Went in this room. There were all these mirrors. Lights. Poles. I knew the judges, two men and a woman, were watching me through the mirrors. I was fucking high as a fucking kite. All the lights were kind of jittering around me. For a moment they'd be super clear and then move again. I danced. I took off my clothes like bit by bit. Did the moves Foxy Jennifer taught me. I felt like I was in the mirrors. Kind of like they were part of me."

"Whoa." Dim red light lit her angular face. We were in Mira's room. Lying on two overlapping mattresses on the floor. Talking close together.

"Yeah, then the music stopped. I picked up my clothes. They came out and said, 'I don't think you're really Lusty Lady material. Thanks for playing.'' What the shit am I going to do now?"

"Do you know of any other clubs? There have got to be other clubs."

"There's all those ones in North Beach on Columbus. But God, I had no idea it would be this hard! I thought I could just be sexy just breathing and men would give me money."

"Well, isn't Foxy Jennifer laid up after another epidural now?"

"Yeah, she hurt her back. After twenty years on the pole. She made bank for a long time, though."

"What I'm saying, is that pole dancing is serious physical work."

"Shit. I'm not made to work. I'm made to be someone's girlfriend. Do you have any coke?"

"Here," I disappeared into my room and came back with an almost-empty bag. "We can shake this for dust and I think get a couple lines out of it." Was giving her drugs my way of trying to get me to be her girlfriend? Or were we just friends?Glamorous phantoms.

Tank was impressed by my victory. Getting E for both of us. He let me come with him, again, to the Westin.

"It's like, I don't like taking you dangerous places like this. But I see you're getting good at the con yourself. You're so subtle."

I was so proud of myself. Finally picking it up. I wanted to get something for nothing like my friends. I could work as many hours as possible at these temp jobs. I would still get thrown away like the trash. Once my two weeks or two days were up. Whatever arbitrary threshold they had for my utility. The money was never enough.

I wasn't graceful or brave enough to be a stripper. Angelina was so much prettier than I was. If she failed, I just couldn't see myself succeeding.

Mira and Angelina used baskets at Sephora. Threw in whatever make up caught their fancy. Paid with stolen gift cards. My makeup was from the drug store. My eyeliner blotched. Broke. Their eyeliner glided. Gilded.

I knew that Mira and Angelina were criminals. I was scared of going to prison. Tried not to get involved.

Mira had done time. She rarely talked about it, except to say, "I taught them all Double-Dutch. They loved me." She acted like the two years she spent in the big house were just a lark. I didn't want it.

Tank and I showed up at the Westin that morning. My ears and mind open to what I could learn. My nose hungry. The porn played with the sound on low. Only Jeff was in the lavish hotel room. He ate some Thai take-out.

"Hey, can you guys come back in like twenty? I want to eat and chill out for a little bit before we do this."

I looked at Tank, "Coffee?"

"Yeah. Coffee."

We took off, heading to a Starbucks on Third and Market. Relaxing brown walls. I poured more coffee,

It was eight am. We were up all night. As was usual. Coffee after speed always felt like a second wind. With a gentler hand. I was getting good at chasing the drip around the globe of a pipe. Too good.

Ben came over to our flat off of Haight. Sat with me in Mira's room.

"Are you okay?" He said. Don't you think you're doing too much meth?" Ben said. "I mean, it's been an everyday thing for a few months now."

"It's just a few months." I answered. "I can change."

"But do you want to change?"

"No. Not really. I mean, what else is there to do?" I looked at him through the smoke haze of Mira's room.

I looked across the table at Tank. He gulped the last of his coffee. "We should head back. I'm anxious to get this done."

"Ok, ok."

We went out under the green awning. Walked down the sidewalk. The street felt carved out of towering stone skyscrapers. We passed a Subway, Dave's Bar and an Office Depot. Crossed Stevenson. A bus rushed by us. Cloud of exhaust. Across the street from the Westin, Tank took my arm. Danger.

"Keep walking," he said in a low voice. "Don't look. Don't cross the street. We're getting a cab in two blocks, okay?"

I heard the eerie whine of a police car. From my peripheral vision as I sipped my iced coffee in faux-nonchalance. Six cop cars in the Westin's drive-in entrance.

Back home in the Haight, I sat on the couch. Dave fussed with the remote. We watched Adult Swim. I wasn't talking. Didn't know what I saw meant. For sure. Hid my worry in with a beer. Bong hits. Courtesy of Dave. We had never talked much. Until now.

I quivered. On the edge of realizing that I could have been in that hotel room. When the police came in.

It was refreshing to talk to someone about short stories. MFA's. Ambitions. To talk about having a future.

I didn't know if I had a future. I definitely had a past.

The landline rang. Mira raced out of her room to grab it.

"Hello! Oh! Oh my god! Jeff!" She took the phone into her room. I heard muffled voices. Shrieking.

Mira came out. Stood in front of me with her arms folded.

"Well," she said. "Jeff's been arrested. What do you know about that? You were down there today, weren't you?"

"Yeah, I was. Tank and I went in and then went out for coffee. As we were walking back there were cops everywhere. We just got the hell out of there. Missed it by a few minutes, I think."

"Well lucky little you. I wish you had been in that hotel room too."

Angelina came out of Mira's room next. "What the fuck? What the fuck? How are we going to get him out?"

"I kind of don't think we can. I don't have any bail money. Do you have any bail money?" I said. Personally, I didn't know Jeff well enough to spend any of my meagre money on him. He frightened me.

"What about his car?" Mira said. "It's parked at the hotel."

"I can't figure out any way to get that back that doesn't implicate us somehow. And besides, even if we could get the car, we'd have to pay the parking fee for the hotel. It's probably huge. But we're not him. We don't have the little ticket we'd need. It just wouldn't work."

"My god, you guys are a bunch of losers when it comes to breaking people out of jail," Mira said. "If we put our heads together we can come up with something!"

"Oh, yeah. Tweaker plans. Those are always the best," Dave said.

"Why don't I call the police and explain that we need to get his car back and ask how we can do that?" said Mira.

"Are you fucking insane?" said Angelina. "Don't do that! It'll be ten minutes and a car will be here too to arrest us as accomplices. We don't want to show we know him or that we have anything to do with him. We are definitely not calling the SFPD for any reason. Do not do that, Mira. I forbid you."

Dave left. Walked into his room with a slump to his shoulders. I knew it meant unease. He usually talked about the struggle to get material while working an office job. The actuality of true crime in the living room? Not conducive to domestic serenity.

Ben did miniature lines of speed with Mira and I. After a few hours in Mira's room with the red lights on? He was higher than I'd ever seen him. We were all talking fast. Feeling good. Angelina came in. Ben dished out another line for her.

"Now that you're here, there's something I've been wanting to say for awhile," he said. "It's about Billy Vegas. Now I've known him for a damn long time. I've been around in the San Francisco glam scene for a really long time. Billy's been around as long as I have. The man is not twenty-five. He's more like forty-five. Sure he looks good. He looks real handsome. He has a way of reinventing himself every five years or so that he doesn't get stale."

"Really?" said Angelina.

"I hate to tell you this, cause I know you have a thing for him, but he's a fraud. You know that record company he's always talking about that he's signed to? Main Man? That he records with in Scotland?"

I looked at Angelina. I could tell from her face that she knew how high Ben was. She wasn't taking him very seriously, I could tell. I was.

"Yeah, well I looked them up on the Internet. There's no trace. They don't exist. He actually goes home and works at his father's construction company, I think, when he says he's recording. Now I've known Billy for a long time. I mean, we're friends..."

"If you're friends, then why are you talking so much shit?" Angelina asked.

"Because I think you deserve to know what's really going on. Billy also has a serious cocaine problem. Like, he steals coke. Acts like he doesn't have any when he does. To get bumps from others."

"Like, don't we all have serious drug problems?" I said, "I'll be the first to admit I've got one." I didn't mention Angelina. The stolen E. My complicity.

I had to shift the focus away from Billy. Loyalty. There was a tendency, when doing coke. Or speed. With others. To circle in. Gossip. Talk shit. Shifting subjects until our social circle was exhausted.

"You have a drug problem, Lena," Mira said. "I use speed to medicate for my ADHD. It's the same shit as Ritalin, so it should help, right? It's medicine for me. It's different from just a drug problem."

"Yeah, you just have a problem." Angelina said to me. "Or maybe you are mental, like, are you? I know we've never talked about this."

"I'm Bipolar, actually." I said. "I had a psychiatrist say I was before in Portland. I looked it up. I totally fit the signs. I'm on medication but it's not very well monitored. I don't have good health insurance like I had it in college. I take a metric shit ton of medication. I medicate with coke now against the depression too. If I can be manic all the time, that's cool."

"Oh... That's cool. Angelina said coldly. "I do drugs for fun, like, what they're actually for." I had a cold feeling in the pit of my of my stomach.

The landline kept ringing. Jeff kept calling.

"I don't know what he expects us to do for him. Like, we don't have any money! We can't get his car. Like is he calling up just to talk to Mira?" Angelina said, "She's cute, but we really can't help him."

Dave took it much harder. He assembled Mira, Angelina and I in the living room.

"Listen, I've been giving this a lot of thought. A house where felons and drug dealers call night and day is not the sort of house I want to live in. This is my lease. Therefore I am letting you know that you are on very thin ice.

Angelina: you need to find a place to live that is not my couch or housemate's floors. It's been four months. You've been here too long. Stop stealing my spoons.

Mira: your friends are criminals. I'm beginning to think you are too. Keep it where I can't see it. Keep these lowlifes off the premises.

Lena: I feel like you have something going on, but you have a serious drug problem. Your boyfriends are disgusting. Try to work more than you party. Please don't leave any more dried up condoms by the bathroom sink. What you do for a living doesn't bother me, but don't read your writing out loud in the middle of the night."

"Whoa," Angelina said.   This was more judgment than we had ever heard out of him.

Dave continued, "You need to tell this Jeff guy not to call here anymore. There's obviously nothing any of us can do. It makes me very nervous to have prisoners calling the house. I smoke weed too. I also do an illegal thing. You're making everything a lot more dangerous for me.

"Please, try to use common sense and common decency. Not this screwed up, drug addict 'I've lost all perspective, I'll just run around naked and paint the walls' behavior I've been seeing. I don't want to be mom. Or Dad. But I will evict all of you. If things continue like this. Okay?"

I nodded. We all nodded.

The phone rang.

Tank called me. Asked me to meet him on the street. Halfway from the bus stop. There was desperation in this voice that I hadn't heard before. Slurring consonants. A whiskey drawl. An anguish in his tone. He said he'd explain when he got there.

I walked alone down Haight Street. Away from Golden Gate Park. Past Amoeba. Wasteland. Striding onward.

We met on the street. His hovering arms in the darkness. Leering. Outstretched arms gripping across the intersection of Caledonia. He grabbed onto me. Cried on my shoulder that his baby mama was taking his little girl to Boston.

I held him on the street. In the night. Warmth of streetlights flickering. A man walked slowly past muttering, "Outfits, outfits." The concrete pockmarked with gum. Bottle caps. Black smears I couldn't figure out.

"Could you follow them? So you could still see your daughter?"

"I don't know anyone that will take care of me for free. So no, I can't go to Boston." He was hysterical. Wasted.

"Come back up with me." I pulled Tank by the hand. Up the stairs to our apartment. The brown building with red trim. Muted in the dark.

Angelina and Mira clucked around him sympathetically. In the end, there was nothing we could do. I made a bed for him on the couch. Left him there.

Chapter 14— SAN FRANCISCO SOUR

My small rented bedroom. I replaced the bamboo shutters with translucent green chiffon curtains. Plastered paintings and magazine clippings over the "Wall of Fame." Tucked my record player onto a delicate seventies table.

Dave, Limone and I sat in my room talking about Mira and Angelina.

"Here, try this." I put on The Make-Up, "Destination Love." The bass groove slid into gospel exhortation. I said, "It's like, we all used to be such good friends. I feel like things have shifted. I don't know. It freaks me out. I thought I could trust them. But I remember when I first met Angelina. She told me not to trust Mira."

"I remember when you guys moved in," Dave said. "I admit I was sort of naive. I just thought, 'Cool girls. Okay, the one's a little hyper. They're both marginally employed. Let's just see how this goes.' I had an idea this would be so interesting. I didn't realize how deeply criminally involved Mira was."

"Thanks for giving us a chance. I was in a really bad position. I really needed a place."

"Yeah. I've learned some things. Material, I guess. Which reminds me, I'm sort of curious... Don't tell the girls, because I'll totally lose my moral high ground, but, like, do you girls have any blow? I want to try it. I've, like, been around it so much now that I just want to know what the big deal is. You guys always look like your having so much fun."

"Oh my God, really?" Limone said.

"Oh course," I said, 'I'll hook you up. Dude, this is my favorite thing. Just don't blame me if you get really into it. It is really addictive. But it's hella fun, of course. End PSA."

Dave laughed. "I accept your disclaimer. Let's go."

I opened my desk drawer where I kept my stash. Pulled out a half-full baggie of coke. I had taken to storing empty drug bags in my dresser drawer. I once pulled out and counted all the empty drug baggies. A bad feeling.

I took a break from writing *Jet Set Desolate*. That afternoon, with Dave and Limone. Pulled out a hand mirror. Poured out a little pile. I lined up two lines with my library card. Pulled out half a deconstructed pen casing from the drawer.

Money was dirtier than what we were doing.

The sun shone through my pretty green curtains. I held the Bank of America pen tube out to him.

"Oh, you go first." Dave said. "Show me what to do."

I bent down. Held the tube to the tip of the line. Drew it across. Inhaled. I tilted my head back. Sniffed it in deep with a rush of spangle and strobe.

Dionysian: in sin, together.

I smiled. Shook my head from side to side. Handed Dave the tube. He complied.

"Oh! Oh I see! So that's what this is like."

"You like?"

"I think… It's... So awake! So agitated and then... More?"

"Oh sure. Let's have another. That's kind of how it is. Some makes you want more. You have to pace yourself or else you get super high like really quickly. Then you run out and are awake wanting more all night long."

"Oh shit. I'm going to be awake all night, aren't I?"

"Yeah... That's pretty likely. It helps if you have writing or like, projects to do once everyone goes to sleep. I'm one of those people where I'm always up later than everyone. I write, sometimes. When I'm high. I'm sure it's shite, but it gives me an outlet. Makes me feel productive."

"Or we can talk. I want to talk so much."

I put on a Ladytron CD.

I came through the apartment door. Home from a finished temp job. Walked through the living room to my room. Noticed my door was open. I usually kept it closed. I threw my purse on the couch. Went into my room.

Mira was trying on a black chiffon blouse.

"I've been going through and taking back some things that I think are mine," she said.

"What the hell? I wouldn't go in your room and go through your shit."

"Like this one. This is BCBG Maxazria. You wouldn't own something this nice. I would. I'm pretty sure this is mine."

"My friend gave me that before she left town. She used to work there. Fuck you. Take that off."

Mira pouted. Took my friend's black BCBG knit blouse off roughly. I winced for the delicate fabric. It was already weakening on one armhole.

"And this, this I'm sure is mine." She held up another black knit blouse, also BCBG. "I remember lending this to you. I'm taking it back."

"Alright. I don't remember that one but get out. Don't go through my shit."

Mira left. Flounced out on one bare heel.

I sat down at my computer. Realized that the wallpaper changed.

"Oh, I used your computer," wafted in from down the hall from Mira.

"Oh you did? This is also my stuff. You don't have permission to use this."

"I don't have one. It's not fair that you do. You only have one because Daddy bought it for you." Just because my parents had more money then her parents didn't make me responsible for taking care of her. I used to believe that my privilege did guilt me into needing to take care of other people. I finally had to knock that off.

I scrolled. Saw that my cursor had been replaced with a syringe. The start menu was on the left side. Some of my icons were missing. There were new files on the desktop.

"Look, if you're going to use my computer, could you at least not personalize my settings? Just get in. Type or print whatever. Get out? Like don't change up my wallpaper and personalize everything? This isn't your computer. You're a guest on it."

"I like to make things my own."

Mira got worse. I came home to her pert blonde head. Tipped sideways as she looked for the perfect word. Finishing a MySpace message. On my computer.

Mira was not educated. She asked me to type up her MySpace profile. I obliged.

Now Mira posed as twenty-five to her thirty-one on the Internet. Slenderizing lens on her video camera. She took stills of herself. In a corset and blonde ponytail. Put the photos on MySpace. Got a lot of messages.

"How am I supposed to keep up with my admirers if I don't use your computer? You don't mind, do you? I mean, I know you must get messages too."

I got MySpace messages. Mostly from couples looking for a third in a threesome. I marked on my profile that I was bi (true) and a swinger (as a joke). That was asking for trouble. I never responded to those messages.

I communicated with Dustin and his porn people through MySpace. MySpace was business correspondence. To talk to editors. Dustin and I surfed profiles of potential models. Make plans to meet. Revise my erotica. Blow some lines. It was always my job to score. I was running out of money. Warhookers paid twenty cents a word. I received a $500 paycheck that paid my rent one month.

Writing Internet porn was a job, as the temp work slowly dried up. As the first dot-com book busted. As time passed.

Writing erotica was much more fun than office work. I was better suited for it. I should have charged Dustin for the blow that I was covering, though. Came with the territory. It was sex work. After all.

I found myself more and more attracted to Dustin. Natural when laboring over the finer points of how to phrase a cum shot. I would get all hot and bothered. Dustin was invariably a gentleman. He would put me to bed on his mattress in the attic room after one of our work sessions. Disappear downstairs to the couch.

Dustin's good boundaries preserved our working relationship. He was smarter than I was on that point.

I used to believe I could defy the odds, "Things won't get weird. We don't have to let them get weird." I played this hand over and over. Never slept my way up to the top. The top wasn't where I was going.

Sacred prostitute of the artists. Mary. Maria. How do you solve a problem like Maria. Mary Magdalene rising within me. She rose and got her way.

I left things with Dustin as they were. A hyper-eroticized medium. It was my first paid writing job. I finally felt real. I didn't need to sleep with him to seal the deal.

I began to learn. It is not necessary to sleep with people. Or supply people with alcohol. Or drugs. To work together. Boundaries.

I had my twenty-ninth birthday. No check or cash bearing cards arrived. I updated my mother with my address months ago.

I ordered a new set of planner pages. For my Franklin-Covey planner. A ridiculous expense at $50. What the hell did I need to micro-organize?

Crystal meth with Angelina: 4:30 am Mon.

Write with Dustin, 5:45 pm Tues.

Wash dishes: haha never.

Reassure Dave: daily 3:14 pm."

I ordered the planner pages in the faint hopes that I would get another office job. They never showed up.

I blamed Mira. I blamed Mira for the little things like lipsticks and earrings that kept disappearing from my room. I started locking my room when I wasn't home. I started locking my room when I was home.

Persephone goes into the underworld. Eats of Hades' pomegranate. The seeds stick. She must go again and again to the underworld. Taste of the fruit. Winter for a time until returning to spring and summer on earth. I go in and out of the underworld tasting of it's fruits.

Finally, I lost it. I marched up to Mira's door.

"Listen" I said. "I know you've been stealing my shit, Mira. This isn't cool at all. I thought we were friends."

"You're not my friend. You're disgusting! You're a skank with dried up condoms all over your room!"

"You wouldn't know that if you weren't in my room all the time. Isn't your room big enough?" Her room was twice the size of mine. Decorated with Ben's mannequins and record covers.

"I didn't take your shit!"

"Then where did it go? I was supposed to get birthday checks. My aunts are saying they've been cashed. I never saw them."

"Maybe you were on too much coke and you forgot."

"Maybe you fucking stole them. And my Franklin-Covey Planner pages. You fucking stole those too!"

"Why the hell would I steal planner pages. What the hell am I going to do with those?

"Just to fuck with me. Just to be a bitch."

"I'm not a thief."

"Evidence shows otherwise."

"Just eat your rotten chicken."

I lived off of bags of frozen chicken and Rice-A-Roni. Two hours before dinner. I put two chicken legs in a tub of water. To defrost for an hour. Put them in the oven. On a cookie sheet. With some bottled marinade. For forty-five minutes.

Every day. After the chicken was in for about fifteen minutes. The fire alarm would go off. Mira would run out of her room screaming. Run around the apartment in circles while I opened windows. Waved towels at the fire extinguisher. Despaired.

Foxy Jennifer called. I picked up the phone. "Do you, Angelina and Mira want to go to Amnesia tonight?" she said.

"Okay, yeah." I didn't mention that Mira and I were yelling at each other. Angelina was increasingly cold.

Foxy Jennifer picked us up in her Camaro. She wore a denim jumpsuit with a zipper down the front. She was in San Francisco for the week. Staying with her mom outside the city. It was time to party.

Whispering to Angelina, Foxy Jennifer sat us in the elite back booth. I sat next to her. She turned away from me. Mira on my other side kept getting up to manically hug people. Run to the bathroom with them. Mira came back. Shoved herself next to Angelina. Scowled at me. The club was dark. Sparkles of light fell through. Dusts of strobe on Angelina's fur collar. Glints on Mira's bare shoulders.

I was alone.

I was the most alone surrounded by people. Bodies moved through the light. Sixties soul played. Mullets and scarves shone over gaunt chests. I was looking through the darkness for someone to connect with. I would have gone home with anyone.

Foxy Jennifer turned to me. "You guys aren't friends anymore, huh?"

"Things have turned that way. Yes."

"I see. They're complicated girls. Angelina doesn't like anyone getting in her space."

"She's in my space all the time. It's my apartment she's living in."

"Yours and Mira's. Well, I've had friendships go sour. Sometimes all you can do is hold on for the next one."

"Yeah, I guess so. Is it always going to be this way?"

"It gets better, as you get older. People change. They begin to forgive." That struck me. The words fell from her coral lips. I realized she was mentoring me in a way few women took the time to do. For a moment I soaked her in. I appreciated her. I didn't know her. We were two ships, passing in the night.

Chapter 15 — I'M LEAVING, I'M GONE

The call came at four am in early 2005. Tank's voice low on the phone. Almost a whisper. "Come to the Ramada Limited in SOMA, I've got stuff. We can hang."

"Okay. I'll see you in ten."

I got a cab. I was bored. It was something to do. I hadn't seen Tank in a few weeks. The prospect of free speed and possibly sex was at least something to do. Instead of stewing in the failure of my friendships.

I pulled up to the Ramada Limited. Got out of the cab. As the cab pulled away I felt suddenly very lost. Stumbled a little on the cheap mules I purchased months ago at Buffalo Exchange. What was I thinking that I could walk on backless shoes with high heels? I kept walking right out of them, painfully. High heels were an imperative in my subculture, but such a lie.

I limped into the motel warren. Looked for room #217. I found it behind an ice machine. A beige stucco maze. I knocked. Tank answered the door. He looked tore up.

"Hey."

"Hey."

I realized at that moment that I wasn't sure what I was doing there in this cheap hotel room. I wasn't attracted to Tank anymore. The missing tooth and Q-ball head didn't work their magic anymore.

I followed him into the motel room. Took the pipe he offered. A few hits into it he kissed me. I followed him to the bed. We half-heartedly fooled around but he lost his erection. Tank fell asleep.

I couldn't sleep. Coke that morning at home. The meth just jacked me up more.

I paced around the hotel room. Realized a hooker, or another woman with sex on her mind was there before me. There were condom wrappers. A dildo box. Piles of make-up in the room. I considered stealing the Chanel lipstick. Decided that would be wrong. I didn't like to steal. It probably had a disease. I probably had a disease. I was a whore like the one who had been here before me.

Light came in the window. I was naked in the motel room. Pacing around picking white specks out of the carpet. I was disgusted with myself. Got a cab home.

I didn't see Tank again. Didn't want to see him. Closed myself off from as many people as possible. Walled myself in.

San Francisco. As it once was. Will never be again. Still lives. In my mind and books. So I know I'm not alone. I type into my MacBook Pro in the limited abstraction of iCloud storage. My life's work that the revolution. Or Internet shutdown. Or apocalypse. May destroy.

I hope this message reaches you before that. I am sending forth a message in the night. To you on the page.

If you knew me once. I am no longer with you. A memory. Every relationship has a lifetime. This is fiction. Fantasy. Imagination. After all.

I will do. Some. Things. To entertain you. Not. Other things. Boundaries.

I set the line.

I use your eye. To bear witness. To heal. To validate. Alone.

I cast this novel out.

I survive. The work survives.

Cruelty and kindness. Always.

THE END